"'How are you?' sounds sh[allow when dealing] with cancer. *These Clouds [We So Much Dread* is a] transparent and realistic answer to that question. There is an immediacy in reliving the diagnosis, treatment, life, and death of Vernon Stoltzfus through the journal of Sharon, his wife."

"If you know someone who has cancer, *These Clouds We So Much Dread* will help you understand, pray for, and love their family with a greater understanding. Here is an 'unbearably sad' story enriched by the presence of 'a God who is incomprehensibly good.'"

~ LARRY STONE is author of *The Story of the Bible* and *Noah: The Real Story*. As vice president of Thomas Nelson Publishers and president of Rutledge Hill Press, he has published more than a dozen *New York Times* bestsellers. Like most of us, he has friends and relatives whose lives have been taken by cancer. He misses them.

"We owe a debt to those who not only fight the good fight of the faith but who bother to leave a record of it for the rest of us. *The Clouds We So Much Dread* is a one-year journey, a brief step in the stream of an ongoing life seen through a glass darkly, where God's flashlight-sized circle of illumination on our path must be enough. My favorite parts were the interspersed comments of Sharon's four children --- so real and unvarnished and untheological, and worthy of a small book of their own."

~ANDRÉE SEU PETERSON is a Senior Writer for *World* Magazine and the author of three books: *Won't Let You Go Unless You Bless Me, Normal Kingdom Business,* and *We Shall Have Spring Again.*

THE CLOUDS WE SO MUCH DREAD

Sharon M. Stoltzfus

© 2014 Sharon Stoltzfus

All rights reserved. No part of this book may be reproduced or transmitted in any form or by any means, electronic or mechanical, including photocopying, recording, or by any information storage or retrieval system, without permission in writing from the copyright holders.

Cover design by Gentry Lusby.

Published by Shawn Smucker.

Dedicated to...

My Heavenly Father,
to whom all glory goes

And to my children,
Jedidiah, Tovi, Tia and Kezia,
a reflection of His glory.
It is my prayer that this volume will lead you
to a better understanding of who your earthly father was
and who your Heavenly Father is.

Forward

by Fagel Brooks

I remember the first time that my husband and I set eyes on Sharon and Vernon Stoltzfus, a September evening when we gathered with other parents for the traditional back-to-school night at our small Classical Christian school. It was hard not to take note of them: Sharon, strikingly beautiful, standing with two shy little boys clinging to either side of her; Vernon, muscular and suntanned, with a ready, broad smile, holding their baby daughter deftly in the crook of his arm. We were drawn to them that first evening (in part because of the head-covering Sharon wore, an unusual sight in our particular school community), and we left that brief encounter with the sense that they would be worth getting to know.

During our first visit to their home in Honey Brook, Vernon wasted no time in getting to the point: "What is this 'Reformed Theology' we keep hearing about at school?" My husband and I took our time to outline the distinctives commonly implied by that designation while Sharon and Vernon listened intently. At the end, Vernon said, "That just sounds like the Bible to me!" With this pronouncement, he became a committed student of all things related to the character of God and His work of redeeming lost humanity. He would seek out anyone he thought might be further ahead on the path of Biblical knowledge than he was and winsomely but doggedly pepper them with questions. We always went away from our times together full of wonder at the intensity of his hunger for God, his passion to pursue the knowledge of Him, and his singular focus to apply that knowledge to every aspect of and relationship in his life. We had never known two people so devoid of pretense and posturing, who asked questions with both guilelessness and a complete lack of self-consciousness.

The story of Vernon's cancer and death is, unfortunately, not unique. The scourge of this disease, which the World Health Organization predicts will be a "tidal wave" sweeping the globe in the next twenty years, is played out in millions of homes every year. Vernon battled cancer with courage and died with grace, supported and breathtakingly well-loved by Sharon and a host of others -- but neither his bravery nor her love were entirely rare. Sharon kept a blog during that time, but she is one among countless others who do the same in these strange days in which our thoughts and experiences reach thousands with a keystroke. What has driven me to read and re-read, again and again, Sharon's blog from that year and a half is her poignant ability to communicate the bittersweet juxtaposition of the honest anguish of their circumstances with the palpable comfort they received from their growing understanding of the goodness and sovereignty of God.

As someone with a front row seat to their hard passage, I can testify that I saw neither fist-shaking at the heavens nor postured, pseudo-pious smiles. The tears were real and the joy was real. The enduring memory for me is the visible image of invisible grace: believers suffering under the stroke of the Lord, weeping but upheld by the knowledge of His love. In the many moments when I shrink from thoughts of extremity and loss, I find profound encouragement that the One who sustained them in their weakness and frailty will be able to keep me as He kept them, "sound and blameless at the coming of our Lord Jesus Christ. He who calls [us] is faithful, and he will do it." (I Thessalonians 5:23b-24)

God moves in a mysterious way
His wonders to perform;
He plants His footsteps in the sea
And rides upon the storm.

Deep in unfathomable mines
Of never failing skill
He treasures up His bright designs
And works His sovereign will.

Ye fearful saints, fresh courage take;
The clouds ye so much dread
Are big with mercy and shall break
In blessings on your head.

Judge not the Lord by feeble sense,
But trust Him for His grace;
Behind a frowning providence
He hides a smiling face.

His purposes will ripen fast,
Unfolding every hour;
The bud may have a bitter taste,
But sweet will be the flower.

Blind unbelief is sure to err
And scan His work in vain;
God is His own interpreter,
And He will make it plain.

~ "God Moves in a Mysterious Way," William Cowper, 1773

Summer of 2006. Life was good, life was full. Our children, ages four, six, eight, and ten, busy with the summer bliss of no school, no schedule, pool, and popsicles. My husband Vernon, busy with summer landscaping, came home one day in July with a persistent pain. We were not folks to run to doctors on a whim, but morning left us no option.

Life as we knew it ended that day.

This book contains the journal entries I kept for the next year and a half. While some minimal editing has been done, most was left as I wrote it. There has been no hindsight applied, no rewriting with what was later learned. And nothing was written with the knowledge of what the future held. Although my aim was to be completely honest, out of respect for Vernon and my children I left some things unsaid. Living with a suffering person requires a special kind of grace and God was always faithful.

- Sharon M. Stoltzfus

These Clouds We So Much Dread

Part One
A Persistent Pain

*My personal journal
one week before I created a CaringBridge Journal.*

Friday, July 7, 2006

I have not kept a journal for years. Yet something tells me that we are entering a phase of our lives I will wish to have recorded.

Yesterday Vernon came home in considerable discomfort. We both spent a fitful night in which I was guilty of asking him to get a new night nurse and throwing an ice pack at him. Sigh.

This morning I called his mom right away and she graciously changed her plans for the day so that she could keep the children. We were at our family doctor by 8:00 AM, meeting him as he went out to retrieve his morning paper while still tying his "ice cream tie" which he wore in celebration of Friday.

He performed a thorough examination of Vernon, becoming increasingly alarmed at what he heard and found: unexplained 20 pound weight loss, blood in stool, digestive disorders, night sweats, etc. He drew blood several times - Vernon's calluses causing difficulty for the finger prick - results showing him to be slightly anemic. Liver was extended three fingers below normal. Our doctor, normally a gentle, mild-mannered man, sternly expressed that he had never been as upset with anyone as he was with Vernon for not coming to see him sooner. He called and scheduled an immediate CAT scan.

This is our first experience with the medical world.

Vernon was restricted from any food or water until after the scan, which meant he could not even swallow the pain pills our doctor had given him. We walked out of the hospital around 1:00 and are now waiting to hear from the doctor who said he would call this evening with the results of the blood work and CAT scan.

Saturday, July 8, 2006

This morning came with no word from our doctor. I called mid-morning, leaving a message inquiring as to why we hadn't heard from him, desperately trying to assume that no news was good news. He finally called back this afternoon, apologizing for not calling sooner, admitting he had been too afraid to look at the results! He told us that, from his office exam yesterday, he had been confident that Vernon had cancer.

However, the radiologist report stated that the enlarged area in Vernon's liver did not look typical of cancer, yet the radiologist was unsure what it was. He now wants Vernon to see a gastroenterologist for him to view the CAT scan. I called my brother Don in Michigan, who is also a physician, and he was in agreement with all our doctor had said.

Monday, July 10, 2006

    Vernon spent much of the weekend laying on the couch, wincing in pain whenever he moved. He did attend men's prayer breakfast Saturday morning and church Sunday morning and put on a good front. He kept insisting he would be better tomorrow and able to go to work. In his frustration with his condition and discomfort, he is impatient with the children, and this is so unlike him. He finds it difficult to get comfortable in any position, which makes even reading undesirable. I rub his back often.

    We were told that pain from an enlarged liver radiates to the back shoulder blade. I find myself unable to know how to best meet his needs. I am ashamed to admit I find myself easily irritated and resentful with this husband who is not the strong man I am used to. I know the children feel the situation; they seem to be extra naughty... or is it just that Vernon and I are on edge with this unknown?

    I have such fears that threaten to consume me: fears about needing to nurse a husband with a terminal illness... fears of Vernon missing much work and there being no income to pay the bills... fears of mounting medical costs with no health insurance... fears of becoming a widow at a young age and having to rear our four children alone. Frustrated with not knowing how to meet Vernon's needs and sensing the strain on our marriage, I am going to Habakkuk 3:17-19 quite often.

Tuesday, July 11, 2006

    Vernon took his prescribed pain pills and went to work part of the day yesterday, but he regretted that decision later as it heightened his tiredness and soreness. I went to ladies' Bible

Study and had a multitude of errands, so we missed the important phone call from our doctor informing us that our appointment with the gastroenterologist had been scheduled for that very day! It is now rescheduled for Wednesday.

Last night Vernon had a lot of blood in his stool. I'm really getting worried. He has started to take iron and is drinking dandelion tea faithfully. Oh God, the unknown is threatening to consume me, the burden of being strong becoming too heavy to bear. Oh Lord, how often I've reminded others that You will not give us more than we can bear, I cling to that promise now, Heavenly Father. My heart aches to see my husband suffer. I feel guilt about not making him go to the doctor sooner.

But for me it is good to be near God; I have made the Lord God my refuge. ~ Psalms 73:28 ESV

Wednesday, July 12, 2006

My husband left a lovely note on the counter this morning for me, especially sweet considering he slept alone last night after I complained about his restlessness in bed. The enlarged liver is causing him quite the discomfort, yet he says if he could just get that reduced, he'd be fine to work! What a guy!

Well, I never expected to hear what we did at the gastroenterologist today. I could see his mounting concern as he examined both Vernon and the CAT scan. Will I ever forget the image stamped in my head as he wheeled his chair around and said matter-of-factly that he was confident (yes, confident!) that Vernon had cancer in the liver, stomach and colon. I sat there fiercely pinching myself to keep from bawling uncontrollably. My dear husband who had just received a death sentence was the one turning to comfort and console *me*. What a man!

Vernon is now scheduled for an endoscopy and colonoscopy on Friday, a liver biopsy possibly after that. I am a basket case clinging to a Sovereign God. The memory of my mother's horrific battle with cancer is all too fresh.

We had a prayer time with the children when we got home. Vernon went out and threw ball a bit with Jed tonight despite the liver pain; he'll undoubtedly pay for that activity. One starts to treasure each moment together. It's hard not to let one's imagination run wild. Vernon also played a memory game with Kezia. Later that night Vernon's parents came up to visit, which was meaningful.

Thursday, July 13, 2006

Today Vernon is allowed liquids only in prep for the complete emptying of the colon for the tests scheduled tomorrow. Vernon's night was restless once again. He has various pains and usually gravitates from our bed to the couch to upstairs then back again. I was exhausted and woke up this morning with swollen eyes and a headache. I need to get a grip on myself! I am constantly weeping. I know it is not good for my husband or my children for me to be in this emotional state. Sigh.

Our pastor came this afternoon and that was a blessing to both Vernon and me. Although he tried to downplay the actuality of this being cancer, I can't get the earnest dread in the voice of the doctor yesterday out of my head.

A family member, when told of the news of Vernon's cancer diagnosis, said: "Well, it's not the end of the world." I must confess that, to me, it feels like it is.

Cried with my dad on the phone this morning, remembering my mother's eight-year battle with the breast cancer that eventually ravaged her body. The stress of that journey aged my father's countenance dramatically and I feel like I am already beginning to look haggard.

I am sharing in Vernon's sufferings by consuming only liquids with him today in his prep for test tomorrow.

Sovereign Commander of the Universe,
I am sadly harassed by doubts, fears, unbelief...
I sink in deep mire beneath storms and waves,
in horror and distress unutterable.
Help me, O Lord,
to throw myself absolutely and wholly on thee,
for better, for worse, without comfort,
and all but hopeless.
Give me peace of soul, confidence, enlargement
of mind,
morning joy that comes after night heaviness...
In my distress let me not forget this.
All-wise God,
Thy never-failing providence orders every event,
sweetens every fear...

~ "Peril" in The Valley of Vision

Friday, July 14, 2006

Grateful for a sunny morning, birds praising their Maker, a rich cup of coffee, and the fact that "Thy Word is a lamp unto my feet, and a light unto my path." (Psalms 119:105 KJV). Vernon awoke with the words to the hymn "God Moves in Mysterious Ways" comforting him.

Talked with my doctor-brother last night. His medical expertise didn't exactly comfort me. I would have liked for him to say there was a good chance this is not cancer and that cancer in the liver is not a big deal; things of that nature. Alas.

Our marriage relationship right now is a sweet communion. Last night as Vernon expressed his love for me, he said it was almost an adoration. And my heart seems to literally ache with the love I have for him. Who on their wedding day ever imagines what the words "till death do us part… in sickness and health" might require of them? I remember telling my father during my mother's last months that watching him faithfully nurse her with such devoted love and patience, I was truly seeing the "in sickness or health" marriage vow being lived out. My respect for my father at that point was immeasurable.

Saturday, July 15, 2006

Once again I was blown away with the events of yesterday. When a doctor comes toward you with a grim face, you just want to yell, "No! Don't open your mouth! Don't let those words come out - it's too cruel!"

Our pastor, Vernon's mother, my friend Marge, and my spiritual mentor Fagel were the faithful friends who waited with us for the results yesterday. Before long, I was called back into the recovery room and kissed Vernon awake out of his sedated sleep. He told me he didn't remember them doing the endoscopy. At this point I was not yet alarmed, but then Vernon asked the nurse how long he'd been in the procedure room and she said "ten minutes." The poor woman didn't realize what she was admitting. We asked her how it could be only ten minutes when they had told us earlier it would take forty minutes for both procedures. Then she told us that they didn't do the endoscopy. Of course we probed "why not?" to which she responded that they found out what they needed to know ten minutes into the colonoscopy, and that was all she was able to tell us.

It felt like a long wait till the doctor finally came with his grim tale. Advanced stage colon cancer. It feels like part of your body begins to shut down when you hear these things. We badgered him with questions in between times of stunned silence. He recommended fairly immediate surgery and went out and found a surgeon who again explained some of this traumatic news, along with the details of the surgery. They both feel that the tumor in the colon had most likely been there for two to three years.

Vernon kept asking for life expectancy. At first the doctor said he wouldn't give figures but Vernon continued to beg him so, finally, he reluctantly admitted that he didn't have any patients with cancer in their liver that survived more than three to four years. Whoa! When we got home, I did some internet research to learn that in his condition, a life expectancy was even less hopeful, as in likely only two years! Vernon and I agreed we wouldn't allow that information to hang over our heads like a death sentence. After all, our God is bigger than statistics!

Vernon is still unable to eat solids to keep cleaned out for the surgery on Monday. I fast with him.

Saturday, July 15, 2006

Vernon did some tractor work today. It bothers him to see all his unfinished outside work, knowing he won't be able to get at it for at least six weeks... and then? We are beginning to learn about receiving grace in daily - even hourly - allotments.

Vernon's mom and I did some therapeutic weeding of the garden together. She is having a difficult time. I mentioned this to Vernon, telling him how hard it is for me to comprehend how I will feel about my children when they are 44. Of course, now my heart bursts with love for them but it seems like part of that is due to their age and innocence.

Vernon response was: "Well, I am still her little boy."

As I was weeding, I thought about the weeds I found thriving under the huge cabbage leaves and how, like them, I am grateful for the "covering" of my Heavenly Father. Though I do pray this cup would pass from me, I do not wish to resist it. I believe it would mar my fellowship with the One who has seen fit to send it. I must always remember who I am and who God is. Who am I to question His ways? I have no "right" to health and happiness. My Savior suffered for me.

Vernon was rejoicing last night that he could breathe without discomfort. Perhaps it's because his stomach and colon are empty and there is less pressure.

Sunday, July 16, 2006

Both Vernon and I dreaded going to church in a way, not wanting to shed tears with every sympathetic hug. We agreed to sit in the back so that not everybody would be looking at us with pity. During church we both broke down. Vernon wondered if our pastor had purposely chosen songs to make us cry. Our pastor then prayed a long, heartfelt prayer for Vernon.

Afterwards there was church potluck in the Gingrich's back yard. A meal never looked so succulent: barbecued chicken, yummy salads and desserts. I had brought jello for Vernon and we drank water. We didn't stay long as Vernon needed to get home to start his pre-surgery meds. I felt like people didn't really understand how the liver involvement impacts the gravity of the situation. And we didn't really want to go around saying it is incurable and the doctors are rather grim about the future.

In the evening, Vernon's family came over and we sat around a campfire. Later that evening, my brother Marcus arrived from New York and also Vernon's sister Liz and several of his nieces came from Indiana. Vernon and I have had bittersweet communion together these past mornings. We lie there weeping and praying in each other's arms before getting up to face the day the Lord hath made for us. These times will always be precious memories to my bleeding heart.

Monday, July 17, 2006

I took a sleeping aid last night to help me sleep (a first). I did indeed sleep wonderfully, but the next morning Vernon told he'd been up much of the night vomiting (side effects of the pre-surgery meds). I felt like such an insensitive wife.

Vernon spent the morning feeling miserable with nausea and dry heaves. The morning flew by for me as I tried to think of what needed to be done prior to a week long hospital venture.

We were at the hospital by 11:00. Vernon's surgery was over in less than three hours. When they called me back to talk to the surgeon, they let all of my faithful "waiters" come with me: Vernon's parents and several of his sisters, Pastor Arrick along with Elder Bearinger, my brother Marcus, and my best friend Marge. They led us to a little room. My stomach was churning. The surgeon told us that they removed a large cancerous tumor along with part of the colon. They also took liver tissue to biopsy, but it was a formality. The surgeon was sure that it would confirm liver metastasis, and recommended chemo to control the spread, to begin as soon as Vernon recovered from surgery. After he left, Pastor Arrick prayed a most meaningful prayer. Then most of us went down to the cafeteria to eat. It was the first I had eaten in six days, but I couldn't eat much. I simply felt sick.

These Clouds We So Much Dread

Part Two
Mysterious Ways

My online CaringBridge Journal entries...

Friday, July 14, 2006

Dear Friends and Family,

Some of you know a little of what has been going on the past week. To others this will come as a complete shock. Trust me, we are in shock, as well.

Vernon has had some health issues arise over the past year, but nothing that we viewed as serious enough to see a doctor. A week ago Vernon developed severe pain. We went to our family doctor. I will spare you all of the details of the various tests and different doctors we have seen. Long story short: Vernon is scheduled for surgery on Monday to remove part of his colon, along with a large cancerous tumor. Cancer is expected in the liver as well, so a biopsy will be done. This is devastating news. Yet our God is sovereign.

Encouraging emails are very welcome. We covet your prayers. We are singing the following hymn quite often lately:

These Clouds We So Much Dread

God moves in a mysterious way
His wonders to perform;
He plants His footsteps in the sea
And rides upon the storm.

Deep in unfathomable mines
Of never failing skill
He treasures up His bright designs
And works His sovereign will.

Ye fearful saints, fresh courage take;
The clouds ye so much dread
Are big with mercy and shall break
In blessings on your head.

Judge not the Lord by feeble sense,
But trust Him for His grace;
Behind a frowning providence
He hides a smiling face.

His purposes will ripen fast,
Unfolding every hour;
The bud may have a bitter taste,
But sweet will be the flower.

Blind unbelief is sure to err
And scan His work in vain;
God is His own interpreter,
And He will make it plain.

~ "God Moves in a Mysterious Way," William Cowper, 1773

These Clouds We So Much Dread

Tuesday, July 18, 2006

    Whew, what an exhausting day! We checked into the hospital at noon. Vernon arrived in his post-op room at 9pm. It's after midnight and I just got home. I know many of you are faithfully praying us through this day and I owe you an update. First, I want to thank each one of you who has sent an encouraging email. They have meant so much to both of us. They are all printed and in a box for re-reading, for repeat encouragement. I apologize that I cannot respond to each one in a meaningful manner but please know that we thank you much for your prayers, your love, and your offers to help.

    The surgery was "successful." A large, apricot-sized tumor and eight inches of the colon were removed. All of the cancer surrounding that area was removed. Praise God, the colon was reattached. Unfortunately, cancer in the liver was confirmed. We were told there is no cure. Chemotherapy can keep it under control for a while. Yet, with good news and with bad news, as Vernon often quotes: "'Our God is good. Our God is able. Our God is faithful.'"

    Many of you were concerned about me having enough support at the hospital. I had many faithful "waiters" with me. My dear friend, Marge, stayed by my side through the entire eleven hours! Of course, Vernon's parents were there. My brother, Marcus, came down from New York. Vernon's sister, Liz, came east from Indiana. Our faithful pastor, Mr. Arrick, was there. Vernon's sister, Kathy, and numerous more friends dropped in. I was well supported.

    Vernon has an epidural with morphine to enable him to handle the pain for the next three days. He will be hospitalized for nearly a week. Vernon was quite uncomfortable tonight. He has a tube down his throat with a stomach drain, which makes it difficult for him to talk. He was writing notes on a notepad. His nurse told him that he is the first patient ever to come to her care from post-op with a smile. This, we know, is only by the grace of God.

I would like to ask you to pray for Vernon's roommate. He is a nice, young man on a difficult journey of his own.

Blessings to each one of you as we strive to bring glory to God, even through all of this.

Thursday, July 20, 2006

Sorry about the delay in updating some of you folks, especially from a distance, who are waiting on news. When I got home from the hospital on Tuesday evening we had no electricity due to a short but severe storm that blew through that evening. When I got up and left for the hospital the next morning I still had no electricity. When I got home from the hospital last night I again had no electricity, but praise God it came on during the night last night and this morning we are once again able to brush our teeth, flush the toilets, receive and send emails, and the like. We are spoiled in this country but I certainly appreciate our luxuries.

Vernon is doing well! He was up and walking twice yesterday, was able to start on a little clear liquids, and was experiencing a bit of discomfort in his stomach but the medical staff said that was a good thing.

Family brought the children in to visit the last two evenings. On the first night, Kezia, who has only just turned four years old, was frightened and didn't want to get near Vernon with all his tubes etc.; that was hard. On the way home she cried and said she just wanted Daddy to come home. It's hard for her as she, of course, doesn't understand much of it.

Thank you to all of you who have left messages or emails; they mean so much to us! And I know you will pardon me for not replying to each of them personally at this time. Many people are visiting in the hospital as well and that is a welcome diversion for Vernon and me as long as visits aren't too long.

Do continue to pray for God's grace daily. He has promised to provide.

Friday, July 21, 2006

Dear ones who are holding us up to our Father,

Vernon had an extremely rough day yesterday. They tell us it is typical after this type of surgery. He had his epidural removed and sure does miss the steady flow of morphine! He is quite the saint, though; I doubt a nurse ever had a patient tell her with a smile before that his pain was at a number ten. It was a difficult day for both of us. Pain always has a way of wearing you down and we continue clinging to God's grace. I just talked with him this morning and his night wasn't so good either. I usually go in each day for about twelve hours. Vernon's mother has been staying overnight with me.

Pray for our children. They are, each one, feeling the effects of all this.

I don't feel like I have much to say but once again I want to express gratitude for all of your prayers and encouraging e-mails.

Saturday, July 22, 2006

Yesterday I felt like I almost fantasized about what it would be like to go home to just myself instead of also needing to meet the emotional and physical needs of four young souls. I am so incredibly exhausted.

The last two days I believe I have discovered what it means to be a nurse, trying to meet the fairly constant needs of someone who is in discomfort. Vernon really felt horrible the past two days. I literally spent much of both days simply rubbing his back. Last evening he reached the first passing of stool milestone (it seemed mostly clotted blood to me) which seemed to relieve much of the gas pain and then he had a good nap for an hour and when he awoke, he said he felt a world of difference better. It was easier to leave him than it was the night before. I am eager to call him this morning to see how his night went. They removed his IV yesterday so we're hoping for a Sunday release.

I wish I was sleeping now but I've been sleeping with my children (slumber party on the living room floor - they like that) and tonight many of them are waking for this or that and I finally gave up on sleep for now.

My cousin Rose who lives in Chicago came today to spend a week and a half. Vernon and I both agreed that with the unknown of recovery, it might be helpful to have our "nanny" back. She has come to help me with my last two babies' home births since my Mother was no longer able to. The children love and respect her and she blends into our family well. Along with her came, in some sense, a huge sense of relief; her quiet calm and kind control are such a comfort. I don't know what kind of week to expect next week but I'm expecting Vernon could still be in a good deal of pain, and I'm feeling we need to establish some sort of normalcy for the children. This shipping them out every day is the pits.

Family came today to our house and put in a hospital bed and air conditioning in preparation for Vernon's return home from the hospital.

Vernon hadn't wanted the children to come in the last several days since he felt so poorly but I said that I thought they needed it. So they came in yesterday and we had a therapeutic time together, laughing, crying, singing, and praying.

Vernon and I have been singing the songs "All the Way my Saviour Leads Me" along with "God Moves in Mysterious Way" often lately. We've found some halls that are fairly deserted, with no patient rooms, so we spend much time walking. There are many moments when we must simply stop and weep at some of the phrases in those songs. And I must confess that when we prayed "The Lord's Prayer" together yesterday, I stumbled at the words *"Thy will be done"* (Matthew 6:10 KJV).

Do continue to beseech God's promised, sufficient grace. Thank you once again for all your thoughts, prayers, and words.

Sunday, July 23, 2006

Vernon called from the hospital this morning exclaiming in desperation, "Come get me, I've got to get out of here!" His discharge was welcome news! We sang "It is Well With my Soul" through tears on the way home. He is resting now (or attempting to). It is difficult for him to get comfortable. He faces a six-week recovery after which chemo will begin. We don't meet with the doctor to go over the liver biopsy for another three weeks, so I expect we will learn more then.

The children were fighting within minutes of Vernon being home. Their loudness, constant activity, and especially the bickering really irritates him in his discomfort and fatigue, and this is incredibly uncharacteristic of him. He had such bad back pain, he was actually in tears over it. Fatigue and pain combined are killers.

Thank you for all your emails, cards, visits, prayers, and kindness expressed in other ways.

Sunday, July 30, 2006

Lord's Day Greetings! We are very much looking forward to worshiping together as a family this day. Vernon isn't sure what he will wear since loose elastic or drawstring waistbands aren't exactly in style as dress pants.

With some we talk about the "why" of it all and our part in accepting what God has ordained. I would highly recommend reading the book *When God Weeps* written by Joni Eareckson Tada and our friend and former pastor Steve Estes. It is what God used effectively with me when I needed to helplessly watch my mother's horrific battle with cancer five years ago.

Our children are bravely accepting the disappointment of a canceled trip to the waves of Chincoteague in Virginia that we had scheduled with friends this week before God ordered our steps anew.

Tuesday, August 1, 2006

When the woes of life o'ertake me,
Hopes deceive and fears annoy,
Never shall the cross forsake me;
Lo! it glows with peace and joy.

Bane and blessing, pain and pleasure,
By the cross are sanctified;
Peace is there, that knows no measure,
Joys that through all time abide.

~ "In the Cross of Christ I Glory" by John Bowring, 1825

These Clouds We So Much Dread

This is not so much an "update" on Vernon but rather glimpses into our present lives that we offer merely as an aid to your intercession on our behalf. It is both hard and humbling to bare one's soul to so many, and especially to some whom we don't know well. But as Vernon said recently: "In the economy of God we are nearing bankruptcy because of our indebtedness to God and His people."

"I can't sleep 'cause I don't know how, I forgot." Words from Tia (age six) last night at 1:30 AM. Nights. They are no longer a joy, no longer my favorite "time of day." Bedtime now brings with it a sense of dread. Last night was a particularly restless one, even the youngest among us affected. We've taken to drinking hot milk and honey.

Yesterday found us in the surgeon's office to have Vernon's staples removed. He now walks gingerly about held together with tape. They did answer some of our concerns with his swelling and pain as a result of the liver biopsy.

We seek wisdom from above in the next step of the journey. One can easily become inundated with well-meaning folks offering advice and by no means do I wish to be unkind, but it can be quite overwhelming and frustrating sorting through it all. We are pursuing treatment options.

Some of you express well-meaning words of encouragement in how we are handling this "trial" God has ordained for us. And though I greatly appreciate your kind intentions, I feel unrest lest I "set you straight." Yes, it is our utmost aim to bring God glory but I assure you, dear friends, we fall far short of the mark. In this house lives a pack of sinners! There are times our tempers match the July thermometer outside. But as Vernon's brother-in-law Craig wrote yesterday: "Grace to you. I was impressed this morning in reading Dallas Willard's *Renovation of the Heart* that mature Christians are not those that need less grace, but those who consume more grace. I suppose that your constant imbibing of grace over the past weeks is a great growth hormone, so to speak. So, again, grace to you."

My cousin Rose, here to help this week from Chicago, is a psychologist and we often joke about our needs these days for therapy. She has been helpful in a myriad of ways as she has selflessly devoted her time to us.

"Give us this day our daily bread" (Matthew 6:11 KJV), our Savior hath taught us to pray. We receive with gratitude the ways our Heavenly Father is providing through His people. Just yesterday I thought how nice it would be if someone would keep me supplied in bread. Should've I been surprised when last evening on our doorstep appears Vernon's niece with three loaves of freshly baked whole wheat bread? That is only one of the multitude of ways God has keeping the oil in our jar filled. What was that again? "Our God is Good, Our God is Able, and Our God is Faithful." Amen!

Wednesday, August 9, 2006

Greetings again. It's been a bit since I've sent an update and honestly that's because I didn't feel I had anything positive to share. We've had some real low spots this past week. One teary eve, Vernon sang to me "Great Is Thy Faithfulness" and I am ashamed to say I had to ask just exactly *what* mercies are new every morning (other than that another dreaded night is over).

We just returned from our surgeon visit. He really didn't tell us too much new news. The cancer is spread extensively to both lobes of the liver and since it was found in the lymph nodes as well… well, you know how scary that is. The discomfort and pain Vernon continues to experience in his right side of his back is related to the liver. We now need to actively pursue the next step in the journey which will be with an oncologist to begin chemo. We are trying to get into Fox Chase in Philadelphia. Could you pray that God would lead and direct and open and close doors accordingly? Could you also pray for Vernon's nights, that he would be able to rest better?

This last week has also been a trial with sickness in the girls and me and we are also praying Vernon will not catch it, as that is the last thing his immune system needs.

Away, Despair! My gracious Lord doth hear:
Though winds and waves assault my keel,
He doth preserve it, he doth steer,
Ev'n when the boat seems most to reel:
Storms are the triumph of his art:
Well may he close his eyes, but not his heart.
~ George Herbert, 1633

We are clinging to the Maker of the waves.

Thursday, August 10, 2006

From the pen of Vernon:

Mercies... new every morning? Yes, and even at night. The moon following its course across the heavens on a night punctuated by sleeplessness - reminders of God's power and faithfulness and light as it waxed to its fullest degree.

"Send forth your light and your truth, let them guide me, let them bring me to your holy mountain to the place where you dwell." (Psalm 43:3 NIV)

Mercies... new every morning? Yes, especially those of extra time spent with family. My sons are reading to me from the book of Joshua. Max McLean not yet are they, but a willingness to read slowly, clearly, and expressively brings me pride of them and comfort from the ancient scriptures:

Joshua's conquest was Canaan, our conquest is cancer. "Do not let this Book of the law depart from your mouth, meditate on it day and night, so that you may be careful to do everything written in it. Then you will be prosperous and successful. Have I not commanded you? Be strong and courageous, Do not be terrified, Do not be discouraged for the Lord your God will be with you wherever you go." ~ Joshua 1:8 NIV

Mercies... new every morning? Yes, a morning after the full moon ran its course, and I was reminded of God's sending forth his light and truth. I was given a reading by John Piper and David Powlison on dealing with cancer (five months after a conference on suffering and the sovereignty of God, they were both diagnosed with prostate cancer). The paper is entitled "Don't Waste Your Cancer." The first point they make is: "You will waste your cancer if you do not believe it is designed for you by God." Nine other biblical points as strong follow. It was a mercy, full of light and truth, well-received that day. A parting of the low-lying clouds that sometimes impair our vision of God's goodness.

Mercies... new every morning? Yes. During a recent conversation about my mortality to our family, we discussed the possibility to them of Dad's cancer having spread beyond what we already know; of chemotherapy treatments that might make Dad even more ill. I told them that I believe I will be healed by God. Now, I'm not claiming that, I don't have an inside track on what God is up to, and I am not in denial. But I also told them He might not and might call me to heaven where I'm needed more than here to sing in the heavenly choir. One son tipped his chair over on the floor to cover up his grief. Another sobbed openly. Tia, processing beyond most six-year old comprehension, asked: "Daddy, should we not pray then that you would be healed?" Oh, what sweetness.

Two Verizon commercials have been in our discourse of late, the first being the older Verizon jingle (I believe it is Verizon anyway), the one asking: "Can you hear me now?" I've taken the liberty to remove 'hear' and replace it with 'trust': "Can you trust me now?" Our journey in the reform faith, of course, centers around God's sovereignty - in election, in salvation, in *sanctification, and in the events that shape our daily lives. Now God is asking: "May I take your head knowledge and make it your experience? Can you trust Me now? Can Jed trust Me now? Can Tovi trust Me now? Can Tia trust Me now? Can Kezia trust Me now?"*

The second jingle (also by Verizon, I believe) is: "You've got the network." A truism well beyond Verizon's ability to claim, when God's people far and wide and all their friends, and all their Bible Studies, and all their churches, and all their neighbors, and all their civic groups join to beseech the Almighty for one of his chosen.

Thanks for the network,
Vernon

Yes, God's mercies are new each day.

Pray with us for direction in choosing an oncologist and for wisdom in sorting out all the miracle claims of supplemental foods, hoping to build the immune system with some kind of systematic nutrition. But mostly for a daily intake of the power of the gospel, especially that we be found hidden in its centerpiece: our Lord Jesus Christ (Colossians 3:3).

Wednesday, August 16, 2006

Thank you to all of you who remembered Vernon's birthday. The mailbox exploded with kindness.

This past weekend, Vernon's family took our children camping. Vernon and I enjoyed some peaceful hours at home. During one contemplative and tender time, we pled for mercy to our God that we might yet enjoy the "empty nest" together someday.

We are grateful to have secured an appointment with Fox Chase Cancer Center in Philadelphia next Wednesday.

Saturday night was Vernon's best night; he slept over five hours straight! He still rotates from the couch to the recliner and wakes often. I am sleeping fairly well, just operating on much less sleep than I used to think I required as we go to bed really late now so that we'll be able to sleep.

We never truly know what is mulling in our children's minds. Out of the blue today Tia came to me and questioned: "Mom, is it dark on the inside of you?"

To which I replied without thinking: "Yes."

Tia then asked: "So, did they have to use a flashlight for Daddy?"

We are planning to leave for Chincoteague/Assateague Island tomorrow for two nights. Some friends of ours are paying for our entire vacation. Would you pray with us for Vernon's comfort on this venture especially sleeping at night? Were this not an annual tradition and previously planned, we might not be attempting the trip, but we do not want to disappoint our children.

"Give us this day our daily bread" (Matthew 6:11 KJV). I prayed several weeks ago, and can I tell you we have received more loaves of bread than fit in my freezer! What a mighty God we serve!

And while we are on the subject of blessings, we have been overwhelmed with the gifts we have been showered with. Today a huge sum of money came from someone we don't even know! I hesitate to even begin mentioning the multitude of blessings we received lest I forget some, and I assure you each one is a treasure. From prayers to a recliner to pizza to books to lawn mowing to gas cards to groceries to meals to school supplies. You get the picture: God is indeed faithful, God is indeed able, and God is indeed good.

The body of Christ is... well, beyond description in their expressions of love and care. We are so blessed with the goodness of God's own.

Basking in His goodness.

Sunday, August 20, 2006

I had asked for prayers on Vernon's behalf for our two-day trip to Virginia and many people have been asking how it went. As far as Vernon's sleeping: the room we had included a couch so he was able to get fairly comfortable on that, propped up on multiple pillows. And the room we had... we felt a bit out of our league. It was a lovely presidential suite with a wraparound balcony maybe thirty feet from the waterfront with a gorgeous view. The children were enthralled with the remote control blinds. And there was a whirlpool in our room which we all enjoyed. (Okay, I put in too many bubbles for Vernon!)

One morning as we sat out on the deck in family worship, going through the book of Job, Vernon told the children how, unlike Job's three friends who came and told him he had sinned, our friends put us up in a hotel room like this! It was a bit hard to relate to Job out there as we would pause to watch the drawbridge let the boats go through. Vernon even spent a day on the beach with us, though he only looked at the waves longingly. The children had a wonderful time in the sand, surf and sun. In all honesty, it wasn't a vacation like we've ever had before and I must confess it feels like the days of Vernon and I 'having fun' are over, but we were very grateful for the opportunity to go and I don't think the children were disappointed. Our friends took them along to the beach the second day. I made a navigational error on the way home and it ended up taking five hours.

Vernon, in his discomfort, thought we would never get home, but we did, and there is truly no place like home.

My desire is to be like Job in Chapter One where, after he has been told of all the calamities now upon him, it says he tore his clothes, then fell down on the ground and worshiped. Oh that our first (and lasting) response to hardships could be truly worshiping the Lord!

Worshiping Him together.

Monday, August 21, 2006

We went to the doctor this morning, due to Vernon's increased swelling in his abdomen. He is to go in tomorrow to have fluid drained off. This is due to his liver not functioning properly.

Sober and scared.

Tuesday, August 22, 2006

Vernon and I spent the afternoon at Lancaster General Hospital where he got to wear one of those cute nightgowns again. Having paracentesis done (or in plain English: draining fluid off the abdomen). Unfortunately, I wasn't allowed to observe. The doctor told him he had triplets after they removed 4 1/2 liters, or ten pounds of fluid! So he is feeling much lighter and much relieved from previous pressure. Sadly, this is a procedure that may need to be repeated in several weeks. They are sending a sample of the fluid to the lab to test for cancer cells.

Our appointment at Fox Chase in Philadelphia is tomorrow morning at 8:00 (we live about 1 ½ hours away) and they said to allow three hours for the first consultation visit.

My cousin Dan, currently living in Wisconsin, who had flown in last week to defend his thesis at Princeton, kindly extended his flight so that he could accompany us to our appointment tomorrow. Interestingly enough, his field of study currently is in cancer cell research. He has been a blessing these past days, not only with his wisdom and hands-on help, but his sense of humor has been refreshing to us all. Our children really look up to him, but then they probably get that from their mother.

Vernon had mentioned the article "Don't Waste Your Cancer" by Piper and Powlison in a recent post. Vernon's mother made the comment that it could well be read once a week in a time like this.

Wednesday, August 23, 2006

Just returned from Fox Chase Cancer Center, overwhelmed. We are, however, quite pleased with our doctors and the staff was extremely helpful and kind. The schedule for next week looks quite daunting with four more trips to Philadelphia, but they wanted to get him started as soon as possible. They want to take another CAT scan as well as a whole body bone scan, along with blood work to determine present liver function. They need to have a port installed to begin chemo.

As of now, his treatment regimen will look somewhat like this: every two weeks he will need to go in for an infusion into his port, then come home with a bag to wear that will continue to infuse something else for two days, then go back to have the bag removed. And repeat. And repeat. And pray for God's mercy in chemo side effects and for remission. They have told us there is no cure for his condition. The life expectancy is not exactly cheery but our God does not follow statistics. Vernon told the doctor that he (the doctor) just might get to see his first case of healing. There were moments this morning Vernon nearly glazed over, paralyzed in fear at the prospect of the barrage of "medicalness" that his body will need to be subjected to. Remember this is a guy who faints at the dentist! At one point he had to go on a walk so he could sing a hymn, and the Spirit refreshed his soul.

I am sure everyone who has faced this beast called cancer has needed to answer the questions: "Is it worth it? Is the fight with chemo and all its harsh side effects worth the effort to live a little longer?" But Vernon has a love for his four precious joys that is unbounded, not to mention a wife who is petrified at the thought of life without him.

A country song tells the story of a man recently diagnosed with a terminal illness and how he does things he always wanted to do, such as going skydiving and mountain climbing. I find the song makes me angry. Realistically, how many people actually feel well enough to do those types of things by the time they get the blow of news like that? But then, perhaps I am missing the message in my own frustration over my husband's condition.

Several months ago, before this nightmare began, we had purchased tickets to Colorado for Vernon and Jedidiah to attend Vernon's niece's wedding on Labor Day weekend. It was to be a special time for Dad and son. The doctors today did not recommend the trip. I am dreading breaking the news to Jed.

As a dear and godly friend of ours, Fagel, said to us: "Your lives will be different, because you will have the *illusion* of assuming that you can count on tomorrow stripped away. *None* of us has that assurance, but we live as if we do -- to our spiritual detriment."

How does one react in a time like this? Someone asked me last evening, "What is life like?" I'd say it's sort of like being on autopilot; sort of like living in a daze. The troubles of life that used to seem monumental now have really faded in significance. Weeds and dust collect but that, too, is meaningless.

Cancer... that nasty word that Vernon once said should really be made up of four letters, now slips more easily off the tongue than it once did. At lunch today, we could even joke about drinking the diet iced tea which contained cancer-causing substances. One simply cannot exist in a mode of despair and depression over what would indeed look like a hopeless future without the God we know and love. I don't get mad at God as I would have at one time; I feel like my anger was spent when He brought me through the valley with my Mother's horrific death from cancer and taught me who *He* really is. I am now in submission to Him and can accept from Him what He has asked me to bear. I can trust because I do *know* He *is* able, He *is* faithful, He *is* good!

Of course there are times I feel as the Psalmist did, that my eyes are sore from weeping, that the pit of my stomach feels like it is turned inside out, that it feels like I can't take the sunglasses off on a beautiful day, like every fiber of my being is crying out that this simply cannot be happening to me, this terrifying prospect of living without my beloved husband. But I can dry my tears (again) and rest because I belong body and soul to a God who is "infinite, eternal and unchangeable in His being, wisdom, power, holiness, justice, goodness and truth" (Westminster Shorter Catechism Answer to Question Four).

The mail today brought a timely and welcome blessing. Through tears of gratitude we want to thank the anonymous donor who paid for half of our children's tuition this year at Veritas Academy. For those of you who know Vernon well, his childrens' quality education is of utmost importance to him.

Friday, August 25, 2006

Okay, I really don't want this to become a list of woes here (and Vernon genuinely dislikes the focus to be on his health) but we would appreciate prayers for the following:

Six-year old Tia dropped a large rock on her big toe yesterday afternoon and the entire nail is purple. Causes her many tears.

Vernon is suffering from hives which could be a result of the switch in pain meds, but we need to get that corrected today as he is really itchy. His fluid is also coming back in his abdomen at an alarmingly rapid rate and another tap may be soon necessary. Also pain in his hip is significant. We will be talking to his doctor as soon as we are able to this morning.

Thanks for lifting us up before the throne. We are humbled and encouraged by the many who visit this site.

Friday, August 25, 2006

Well, we talked with the doctor and the moral of story seems to be that they don't know what is causing the hives. Vernon will continue to take Benadryl to help alleviate the itching. We have also switched back to former pain medication.

The doctor would like to hold off on tapping more fluid off the abdomen, due to it taking necessary nutrition away and also that it will likely just fill back up right away anyway. They will evaluate on Monday whether he can endure till chemo kicks in and hopefully alleviates the problem.

Oh, Tia now sports a black eye (from her little sister no less!). And yesterday while our pastor was here, he needed to absolve a physical altercation between our boys. Any more questions about how our children are handling the current stress in the family? Seriously, it's not that bad.

Good news! Two of my brothers and their families are coming this weekend (from New York and Michigan). We have a "to do" list ready for my brothers who like to keep busy. We are all looking forward to them coming; the children are excited about seeing their cousins again. And it is always good to have an "in house" doctor, but especially now.

Saturday, August 26, 2006

Thank God (please, truly do!) Vernon's hives have dissipated and his hip pain is lessened...?

Sunday evening at 5:00 we will be having a small anointing service at our home for family and close friends in keeping with James 5:14. We would invite you to join us in prayer from wherever you are at that time.

Blessed Lord's Day tomorrow.

Monday, August 28, 2006

Good morning. We head to Philadelphia at around 8:30, scheduled to meet with the doctor at 10:30, and then Vernon starts a full body bone scan at 12:30. My doctor-brother is accompanying us to Fox Chase today, then they plan to head home later tonight.

Last evening's anointing was a sweet time. Thank you to all of you who were also in prayer at that time, though not physically present. Our greatest desire is that God would get as much glory and gratitude if He chooses *not* to heal Vernon's earthly body as He surely would if He *did* heal him.

Yesterday's sermon on Psalm 73 was nourishing to our souls. "But when I thought how to understand this, it seemed to me a wearisome task, until I went into the sanctuary of God; then I discerned…" (Psalms 73:16-17 ESV) We must indeed go to God, continually and recklessly abandoning ourselves in trust of Him.

In gratitude for your prayers on Vernon's behalf this day.

Monday, August 28, 2006

Well, Vernon survived the bone scan just fine (lover of medical procedures that he is not!). They paid special attention to the hip; however, we will not know the results for another few days. They are waiting to do another tap (drain fluid) until Thursday before the chemo infusion.

My father and his girlfriend are coming tonight to stay a day or so; am looking forward to that. It was oh, so wonderful to have two of my big brothers here over the weekend. Family is special and Vernon didn't feel bad putting them to work as that is what they like to do best. They completed a driveway bed project for him that was bothering him that he couldn't do. It was hard to keep him off his tractor.

Tomorrow we head back to Philadelphia for Vernon to have a port implanted (in which the chemo will be infused). This is a minor surgical procedure but not one Vernon is anticipating with glee or anything.

Many friends send a Psalm as an encouragement and it occurred to me that the words "scripture" and "prescription" sound somewhat alike. Psalms indeed are a prescription for the soul! Been spending too much time in pharmacy lines of late - got prescriptions on the mind. Seems like after every doctor visit, we come home with three more.

Please, don't take your good health for granted.

These Clouds We So Much Dread

Tuesday, August 29, 2006

>Turbans and hats
>Skin and bones
>Wheelchairs and limps
>Bandages and scars
>Sympathetic smiles and furtive glances
>Somberness and silence
>Vomiting in the restrooms
>These are the sights one sees in a cancer center.
>Couples with no smiles
>One holding the other one up
>Shuffling from infusion room to
>Scheduling to yet another cat scan
>This is the world we have entered
>A world of long halls and white coats
>Of needles and nurses
>Of pills and pain
>Of chemo and radiation
>Of pathology reports and prognosis
>Of heartache and hope.
>This is the picture of sin
>In the soul
>And the devastation it wreaks.
>Oh God, your Son
>You sent so long ago
>Still holds the power to heal
>The power to make whole.
>May we go ye into this sin-sick world
>And share this hope we have within us
>The hope of healing
>And of heaven.

I wrote that one day while waiting hours for Vernon in the cancer center. It can be rather disheartening in there. In a regular hospital, people are there for different reasons, but in a cancer center, it is different; you look at people and wonder where their pain is and how soon you will look like them! We sure do want to spread the fragrance of Christ, though, and exude a joy that is not of this world.

Tuesday, August 29, 2006

Written by Vernon around 3:00 AM when he couldn't sleep last night. I type it now for you...

Our resident doctor left for his practice in Michigan last evening. His wife and family went with him, leaving behind some tired and battle-weary Stoltzfus cousins. Together they spent the weekend bruising bodies and egos while tunneling Dad's topsoil stock, re-stacking paver block and brick into fortified cities.

Sharon's to-do list for her brothers was completely scratched off. However, the wealth of Donald's medical knowledge - to be called upon freely by family - was only scratched on the surface. He rode with us to Fox Chase on Monday to stand beside us and ask questions concerning our medical attention. He gave me advice on eating less, but more frequently, on making what you eat count (celery, for instance, burns more calories than it feeds you), on eating more ice cream. Thanks, Don and Marilee. Thanks, too, Marcus and Bev.

As milestones go, we have now reached the end of our six-week recovery period. Monday was our six-week post-op anniversary. Starting Thursday, we enter the treatment phase of our recovery. Today we visit Fox Chase to put in a port for the treatments.

God has graciously tended our little flock over those six weeks. Thanks to your many generous gifts, our pasture is green and the springs have not dried up. Many times He has shielded our minds from thinking too far ahead. He has, as He promised to do, directed our steps ("A man's heart deviseth his way: but the Lord directeth his steps." ~ Proverbs 16:9 KJV). He has given us a refuge in His Son through song and scripture. He has not given us more than we could bear.

We look to Thursday with both anticipation and trembling. This is our first offensive measure in taking on the cancer. But, somewhat afraid, we enter the world of many unknowns and possibilities. How will my body respond? How will God affect the treatment to His purposes? Will He use it to bring miraculous healing? (May Jesus Christ be praised.) Will cancer be set back, giving at least temporary relief? Probably more likely, what is temporary relief, 1 year, 2 years, 5 years, or 20 years? (May Jesus Christ be praised.) Will treatment have little effect? (May Jesus Christ be praised.)

On Sunday evening, friends, family and church elders gathered at our home to pray and anoint the sick. They came to call upon our Intercessor and His Father to stretch out His hand of mercy on a son, friend and brother. But, as one theologian noted, they did it (as with all prayer) not so much to change God's mind, but to make us ready to receive God's answer. That answer will be made according to the counsel of His will, for His own glory, whereby He foreordained all things to work together for my salvation and the salvation of my family. Thanks be to God.

Many of you have written that we are continually in your thoughts and prayers. We are so grateful for your perseverance in interceding on our behalf.

What you are telling us you're doing for us is a picture of what each of our lives with God should be like! A continued meditation and remembrance of God's law, its truth, His goodness, His ability to save, work wonders, as He reigns until He has put all His enemies under His feet.

Wednesday, August 30, 2006

Okay, okay, people are e-mailing wondering how Vernon is doing after yesterday's procedure of having the port put in. It's hard to know what to say, especially when he doesn't like people to know when and how he suffers. I was a bit taken aback when they brought him out to me in a wheelchair, but it was a minor surgery with anesthesia. He is doing ok; discomfort in that area, of course, but it looks to be healing well. His major discomfort at this point is his fluid in the abdomen which they are scheduled to drain tomorrow before starting the first chemo round.

Vernon is out walking right now with a cane! Oh, this is hard.

God continues to show His goodness in daily increments through His people. We came home last evening to four more loaves of fresh bread on our table and I had been completely out of bread. How did they know other than to be prompted by our daily bread Provider! Also, following a tearful frustrating conversation between Vernon and I concerning future living expenses, what should come but more financial sustenance! I weep and repent over my lack of faith and trust and gratitude in our Maker.

Wednesday, August 30, 2006

They called from Fox Chase this afternoon and want us in even earlier tomorrow morning for hip and femur x-rays. Scary! So now we need to leave at 6:30 AM and tomorrow's full agenda includes the above, then parentesis, then chemo and coming home with bag attached for two more days of chemo. We covet your prayers; looks to be a long, hard day.

Vernon is feeling really rotten. We were not able to attend our childrens' school convocation - first we have ever missed!

Yet another "Let Jesus Christ Be Praised" report as we were able to set up a visiting nurse for the chemo bag removal, so we won't need to make yet another trip to Philadelphia on Saturday.

Thursday, August 31, 2006

Home again, home again, jiggity jig. Home again, home again in our now-trustworthy rig. Thanks to a friend for all the work he did on our broken-down van yesterday!

Our pastor accompanied us to Fox Chase today. Grateful for the raw conversations, physical presence of a friend and chauffeur.

It was a full day, complete with x-rays, paracentesis and chemo. They drained two liters of fluid off the abdomen and assumed there is another three liters in there, but hesitate to take more off as it will just fill up again anyway. And then, chemo, patiently waiting for four more hours of drip, drip, drip. Three drugs there then another one sent home in a bag attached to his port for another forty-six hours (I told Vernon he can find out what it is like to carry a purse, although this is much different as we don't need to be attached to our purses).

They did find cancer in his right femur bone. They don't want to combine chemo and radiation at this point so want to continue the chemo regimen for 4-6 weeks to get the liver and fluid retention under control, then they will want him to do radiation. Meanwhile, they want him to take caution to avoid fracturing the weak bone.

Vernon isn't feeling very many negative effects from the chemo as of yet. We are a bit overwhelmed with all the info we received today regarding life and care of a chemo patient, avoiding cuts and germs and sun, etc.

Do pray for us. We are weary both in body and soul.

These Clouds We So Much Dread

Friday, September 1, 2006

I asked Vernon to write an update for today since everyone is wondering how he is doing and clamors for his writings, but I wasn't successful in persuading him to get a writing accomplished. So…

He really isn't feeling too many chemo effects at this point. He was running a fever today and Fox Chase wanted us to go to the emergency room (a fever over 100.5 is a concern for chemo patients), but Vernon insisted it would come down and it did, actually.

Folks are wondering how he is doing with confirmed news yesterday of the cancer in the bone and the new restrictions it puts on his activity and damper of back-to-work hopes. He says to tell you, "It's no big deal, just one more thing for God to heal."

His restrictions now, though, with the confirmation of cancer in the bone, include not lifting over five to ten pounds! That, and not climbing ladders, etc. That was more than a bit discouraging for him as he was insisting on getting back to work soon.

Today our eldest, Jedidiah, turned eleven. Despite the fact that original plans were for him and his Daddy to be in Colorado this weekend, he had a very happy birthday! The friends who kept him yesterday planned a small party for him, complete with inviting some other boys over so that was a treat for him. And today he was showered with ample attention as well. He received a huge birthday box from cousins in Michigan. Also, a local aunt brought over a birthday cake and ice cream. And Vernon has just committed for Jed to play hockey this fall as some friends have generously offered to pay for it, knowing how much Vernon loves the sport. I think most Friday evenings will be taken up and

I struggle with it a bit, feeling like the last thing I need is a more hectic schedule but Vernon thinks he and Jed need the diversion and I am sure he is right.

In Times of Trouble, God's Trusting Child May Say: He brought me here; it is by His will I am in this strait place; in that will I rest. He will keep me here in His love, and give me grace in this trial to behave as His child. He will make the trial a blessing, teaching me the lessons He intends me to learn, and working in me the grace He means to bestow. In His good time He can bring me out again - how and when He knows.
~ Andrew Murray

Saturday, September 2, 2006

We are off to the ER - fever too high.

Sunday, September 3, 2006

Just got back from the hospital. It's 2:30 AM. More details tomorrow, or I guess that would be today, after some much-desired sleep.

Sunday, September 3, 2006

Vernon wrote the following, I type for him:

Just when you think you're getting good at chemo, a slight twist takes you by surprise. 100.5 body temperature is serious in our new world; anything over that warrants special attention. Friday and Saturday temperatures were in and out of that range almost all day and night: 98, 99, 100, 99, 101. What to do? So, finally tired of pushing the limit, we yielded to better judgement and headed to the ER around 4:00 PM Saturday.

"Where's the emergency?" you've all heard asked when everyone's rushing around. Seems the emergency is lost when you enter the ER. Take a beeper. Wait hours. See a triage nurse and a beeper. Wait hours. Take x-rays and a beeper. Wait hours. Take blood work and a beeper. Wait hours.

Finally admitted, we abandon beeper and wait more hours till blood tests and urine tests results are returned. All turn up fine, but wait - redness on the skin of the scrotum could be fever-causing infection, a condition called cellulitis, not uncommon in chemo patients. Hours of antibiotics later and after waiting for IV nurse to shut down my port, we leave hospital at 1:30 AM. The doctor one way or another was going to evaluate me overnight. He nearly admitted me, but decided not to after talking to other counsel and seeing the countenance fail in his patients.

This God of ours, we don't sometimes like the schedule He keeps but we are infatuated with His mercy: mercy in last-minute child care, not having to spend all night in the hospital, and Lord's Day attendance the following morning.

Monday, September 4, 2006

Well, you could look at it this way, when you come to the site and there is no update, you save time because there is nothing to read, right? Seriously, we are humbled at all the hits this site gets and the people who pour their prayers to the Father on our behalf.

How is Vernon doing? Experiencing some nasty side effects of the strong antibiotic they have him on, also full with fluid retention and swelling, but he is still up and around like an energizer bunny (just maybe a weak one).

Nerves that are dangerously thin of late in Mom and Dad sometimes subject our children to additional tears and hurts. Last night in family worship, we needed to ask our kids forgiveness (not the first time, trust me!) for sinning against them in our irritableness. As Vernon then prayed: "We are not stalwarts of the faith, but sinners saved by grace." If there is one thing we are with our children, it is honest. Honest in our weaknesses, honest in this journey of cancer God has led them on with us, honest in what could lie ahead, honest in our love for them and our Sovereign God who holds us and all He asks us to walk through in His all-sufficient hands. And we take comfort that God can use even our failures in dealing with them (our children) and redeem them for Himself.

Thanks to all you kind friends who remembered my birthday yesterday. Although Vernon didn't feel well enough to go out, it was still special. I had taken the children to the thrift store the day before (to get them out of the house on a rainy day so Vernon could rest) and they had each picked out gifts for me with their own money. So that was really fun and sweet to see what they picked for their mommy. They had remarkably good taste, too, I might add. And my thoughtful husband wrote me a precious note that I will treasure forever.

The childrens' first day of school is tomorrow. Tia is nearly beside herself with excitement as this is the first she goes to school. They are in grades One, Three, and Six. Kezia, only four years old, says she will play with the dog while the others are all away.

God's promised grace to you each day as well.

Tuesday, September 5, 2006

Vernon is feeling the yucky effects of both the chemo and the latest meds. His family is feeling the effect of a sick daddy and husband. The energizer bunny commercial is over.

I'm disgusted with "get well" cards. Did you ever think about how inappropriate the wording is in so many of them?

Realistically, how many times do you send a card to someone with the flu or something ie: "Hope you're feeling better soon..." Gag. How's that sound to the terminally ill? Not implying here at all that cards we've received have had inconsiderate wording; rather, simply frustrated right now as I was searching for cards to send: one to a friend who was recently diagnosed with a brain tumor and bone cancer and then there is another friend (young mother with four children) with recent shocking news of colon cancer.

While we're on the subject of words, might I add some thoughts...

Never avoid a person or situation because of your discomfort. Might I challenge you to get your mind off yourself? And don't feel like you need to be in mourning with them. If there is anything that discourages us, it is people who come expecting us to be in sackcloth and ashes. Vernon has snapped at several (I apologize) who were gushing with sympathy. We truly do appreciate your concern, but it does no one any good to be downhearted about it. Life goes on, we need to talk about things other than ourselves. We will not sit around with a tissue box in our lap on a regular basis. Don't get us wrong; not a day goes by we don't cry out to our Father for mercy, for healing, for strength just to get through the day (or night). There are times we are nearly paralyzed with terror at the thought of the suffering yet to come. But we refuse to let our grief consume us. We accept what God has asked us to bear, not that we don't plead for this cup to be passed from us as our Saviour did in the garden, but recognizing also that we are called to suffer for Him. The following words sum it up well:

My God and Father, while I stray
Far from my home in life's rough way,

These Clouds We So Much Dread

Teach me from my heart to say
Thy Sovereign will be done.

If Thou shouldst call me to resign
What most I prize it ne'er was mine,
All I possess I have made Thine
Thy Loving will be done.

Now let my fainting heart be blest
With Thy sweet Spirit for its guest
My God to Thee I leave the rest
Thy Gracious will be done.

Renew my will from day to day
Blend it with Thine and take away
All that now makes it hard to say
Thy Perfect will be done.

Then when on earth I breathe no more
The prayer oft mixed with tears before
I'll sing upon a happier shore
Thy Glorious will be done.

"My God and Father While I Stray" by Charlotte Elliott, 1834

Wednesday, September 6, 2006

Consider Christian, that all your…
trials and troubles,
calamities and miseries,
crosses and losses,
which you meet with in this world -- is

all the hell that you shall ever have!

*Here and now you have your hell.
hereafter you shall have your heaven!*

*This is the worst of your condition;
the best is yet to come!*

*You have all your pangs, and pains, and throes
here -- that ever you shall have! Your ease, and
rest, and pleasure -- is yet to come!*

*Here you have all your bitters;
your sweets are yet to come!*

*Here you have all your sorrows;
your joys are yet to come!*

*Here you have all your winter nights;
your summer days are yet to come!*

*Here you have all your evil things;
your good things are yet to come!*

*Death will put an end to all your sins
-- and to all your sufferings!*

*Death will be an inlet to those joys, delights,
and comforts -- which shall never have an end!*

*Who can seriously meditate upon this, and not
be silent under God's most smarting rod?*

"All the hell that you shall ever have!" from *The Mute Christian Under the Smarting Rod* by Thomas Brooks, 1659

Thursday, September 7, 2006

> You know your life has changed
> When you're buying face masks and Ensure
> You know life will never be the same
> When you keep a hospital bag packed by the door
> "I Owe The Lord A Morning Song"
> Takes on a whole new meaning when the nights are long.
> You learn that when you are weak,
> Then truly He is strong.
> You no longer take for granted
> The things you used to do
> But in this new journey we to our God's
> Goodness hold true.

I can gauge by the questions in the personal e-mails I receive what I apparently am not addressing on the site...

How is Vernon really doing? While respecting his personal privacy, I will say he is very uncomfortable, dare I say at times miserable. We plead for God's mercy in better days ahead and trust that they will come. When we call Fox Chase about some concerns, they assure us this is typical for the harsh chemo regimen he is on.

I've always thought myself a flexible person but this new life forces one to literally take one day (one hour, rather) at a time as far as making plans, not knowing how he will feel when the event arrives. I apologize to those of you who stop in that are unable to visit Vernon at the time when he is not up to it. Please don't stop coming. And with this new war we wage on germs, thank you for understanding if he must reject a handshake or a hug. And thank you to those friends who put up with my not returning phone calls or not being able to make commitments at this time.

We continue to be grateful for the corporate body of Christ who show His love in so many ways. So grateful for… the hour and a half long massage I received this morning from a friend, for pizza, for floor scrubbing, for lawn mowing and weed pulling, for fresh baked bread or goodies and canned goods, for school lunch treats, for phone bill payments, for mailman surprises, for encouraging e-mails and guest book entries, for prayers for healing and the much-needed daily grace we need to survive.

Friday, September 8, 2006

My mother always taught me: "If you don't have anything nice to say, don't say anything at all." This is one of those days.

Saturday, September 9, 2006

God uses such creative means to nourish my soul: a cricket praising its Maker in the bathroom causes me to stop and join in.

Vernon continues to feel miserable. A large part of his extreme discomfort is due to the high volume of fluid retention. It is likely it will take numerous chemo treatments for the tumor in the liver to be shrunk enough for the liver to start functioning well enough to begin to affect this. This is discouraging. As for negative chemo side effects, we talked with the doctor again today and he prescribed a new medication we will now try in order to help alleviate one particular nasty side effect. However, strangely enough, the pain in his hip has lessened greatly. The site of his cellulitis also seems to be healing nicely. Let Jesus Christ be praised!

How well I'm learning the acid taste self-pity. Last evening I needed to stifle the disappointment of once again missing a looked-forward-to event (our pastor's daughter's wedding).

Those who know me well know me as brutally honest (often to my detriment); therefore, I will not sugarcoat my feelings in this online journal (despite the fact that the vast, perhaps unknown, audience can be intimidating). This is a difficult time for me. I am weary. The stress of seeing my beloved seemingly waste away is insurmountable. I am tired. It is difficult to meet the emotional and physical needs of my four young children. We've always felt it was important that our children be held often, recognizing the importance of physical touch at any age. Rarely does a day go by that one of them does not come to me and say: "Mom, you haven't held me yet today." And I do long to meet those needs, recognizing I need that as well. However, it is challenging to balance being the Mother they need (especially at a time like this) while also being the wife and nurse my husband needs. In painful openness I admit that I am feeling the effects of being a 24-hour nurse with no shift relief. Yet I know that in my beloved's suffering, he needs me, and I want to be there for him. And I do feel a supernatural (God-given) strength during this straining time.

Why do I share all this? People are constantly asking how I am really doing. Were I to answer that honestly on every occasion, it would take too much time and too many tissues. So while I thank you for accepting the answer of "ok", or "good", the truth is it's very, very hard; however, He "hath taught me to say 'It is well with my soul,'" because I know that even though I'm weak, and even though I'm weary, the Lord will indeed "haste the day when my faith will become sight." And, oh how I hate when this starts sounding all about me. Please continue in prayer for Vernon. Pray against discouragement and despair. Pray that each day would be more than just another one to endure. Pray that he could attain nourishment for his body. Also pray for strength in child rearing. At times like this, needed discipline is sometimes neglected for what is easiest and that is not wise. Also, incessant chattering and childish energy can be so taxing. But they truly are our joy and diversion in this time as well.

Late nights and sleepless nights I am reading aloud *When God Weeps* (by Joni Eareckson Tada and Steve Estes) to Vernon. How crucial it is that we are reminded of others whose suffering is far worse than our own. How refreshing it is that the book is strewn with scriptures to back up the theology that in one's physically and emotionally weakened state can be more easily digested. There are so many times I can hardly go on reading, the tears choking my voice.

We continue to bask in the goodness of God's own. This morning on our doorstep was a saint to mow the grass and wash the van. Groceries, meals, expressions of concern, and prayer, prayer, and more prayer are all so dear. We know that we do not walk this journey alone, and we do thank God continually for all of you.

Doing a lot of road running these days between school, music lessons, play practice... May God richly bless the carpoolers in my life this year.

As many of you know, Vernon was an avid hockey player in his prime. It has always been his dream for his boys to play. This fall a friend of ours (another one of the saints we stand in awe of) is making it possible for that dream to be played out in our eldest. It was a hard night a few days back when Vernon wasn't able to accompany his firstborn to his first hockey practice. Although this, along with the other commitments on the calendar, seem like one more time consumption I can't afford, Vernon and I agree the distraction for the children is a positive thing.

Some dear folk commend me for "keeping on" in this difficult time. While I appreciate the words of affirmation and encouragement, I can't help but be slightly amused at the words. After all, what choice do I have? I don't exactly have the luxury of not answering the doorbell (the phone I can ignore, yes) or simply pulling my head under the covers and refusing to meet the new day (though I did think of trying that this morning).

I also find it slightly amusing the amount of people who e-mail me commenting on others' guest book entries on this site, yet they are afraid to post their comments publicly. While we cherish each e-mail or entry, I do challenge you to encourage one another as well.

Sunday, September 10, 2006

Vernon wrote the following this morning: Lord's Day.

Russ, our rooster, woke me about 5:30 AM. He's adamant about his job of calling the new day in - some sort of invocation - invoking upon all near and far that God's mercy has shown through the beams of a new day. As the daylight gains strength, so do his sporadic outbursts: "Praise ye the Lord!" "Praise ye the Lord!"

All nature cries out in manifold witness. The grass greened by four inches of Hurricane Ernesto rain and then manicured neatly by a benevolent neighbor gives witness to the beauty of our natural world - a world spoken into existence by the Great One.

The love that I'm married to... is a love far beyond what I knew when we got married. You all know the sentiment, I'm sure, but wait till life gets real tough; this week I've witnessed in her such fortitude, such strength, such grace as we battled a low week together - never an unkind word, never complained.

Such care, such care, and through it all held up the rest of the family in various activities. Thank you, Sharon.

The kids also, for their part, have made it bearable. Keeping noise outside the house. Faithfully following orders to wash hands. Kezia playing delightfully by herself, when the others are at school.

I count the hours. So many hours till bedtime. When in bed - waking up at night - so many hours till dawn. What to do all day long - concentration is so low so reading is difficult - comfortable seating does not always come readily with abdomen fullness. I lie, I sit, I kneel, I walk (not far this week, rectal accidents occurring frequently), but time rolls by.

We look forward to events, that we need to miss when they arrive: hockey practice, weddings, Lord's Day services, but this too shall pass.

Chemo coming - Wednesday - things will improve - livers working, ascites abating, no virus' attacked, antibiotics course almost over, the wicked pill history.

Monday, September 11, 2006

>Face masks and antibacterial sprays
>Panic at a sneeze
>This is life these days
>Keeping us on our knees
>Recognizing that God too controls the germs
>And we needn't always squirm
>But this current bout of antibiotic
>Makes us to the rules want to stick
>So we ask of you dear friends
>To be respectful to this end
>If you've a sniffle or a contagious ache
>Please do precautions take
>In sharing your well wishes
>We trust you will be judicious

We do not wish to live in a bubble
Yet do want to avoid trouble
Thank you in advance
For helping us keep this precarious balance

Tuesday, September 12, 2006

Vernon felt well enough to take the school children in yesterday morning but came home exhausted. However, after some couch time he was on the road again to help with some design work at a job. He is thrilled to be feeling well enough to get out again. I feel like I am on cloud nine as well! Guess we will adjust to this taking each day as it comes… coping with the bad, living the good ones to the fullest.

We head down to Fox Chase late afternoon for a CAT scan. They just want to check on the liver condition since the CAT scan done nine weeks ago (remember the first day this journey began?). Since we don't know when we will get home tonight and we leave again for Philly early tomorrow morning, the children are staying overnight with cousins. Tomorrow we head down again; this time for doctor visit, lab work and infusion. It will be another long day, then he will bring home his bag buddy for two more days of additional, slow chemo infusion.

So, it's been eight weeks you guys have been hanging in with us. Wow! We continue to be humbled with all the prayers and expressions of kindness towards us. We understand if it's getting old and you put us on the back burner for a while.

Praising God for He *is* indeed *faithful*, *able*, and *good*!

Wednesday, September 13, 2006

Another long day. Time takes on a new essence in doctors' offices and hospitals. Blood work, doctor's visit, chemo room, scheduling, finally home after eleven hours.

Another bout of antibiotics prescribed for a new patch of suspected cellulitis, this time on the abdomen.

Negative news of cancer cells found in the abdomen fluid removed. What this means, we are told, is that cancer is likely in the lining of the abdomen wall. The cancer irritates the lining and blocks the lymphatic system, not allowing it to drain normally. Thus the fluid retention may be more likely due to that rather than lack of liver function as previously thought. At any rate, we anxiously await for chemo to kick in to alleviate this.

Although this revelation comes as a blow, it seems like one becomes numb in this new game of life we now play. Actually I attribute that "numbness" to the anesthetic of God's grace. When I heard this news, my thoughts were: "Well, God knew this too, and if this is His design, my will I can resign."

And as our pastor reminded us recently, God's grace is not like a shot that we receive that lasts all day but rather, as He promises, His grace will be sufficient in the time that we need it.

They had originally scheduled a tap (draining more liters of fluid off the abdomen) today but the day became too full so Vernon needs to head back to Philly tomorrow morning for that procedure. His father will be taking him (our pastor drove us down today - how helpful that is for me to not have that added stress of driving). Vernon anticipates this procedure with joy as it greatly relieves his discomfort. His ankles and feet are swollen to nearly twice their original size and his abdomen - well, today I told him we'll need to start buying maternity clothes for him.

Today Vernon's sisters and mom took care of all children aspects. Also while away, my house was cleaned, groceries left on the table and in the fridge, and supper was brought; thank you to all of you dear people!

In a time like this, I am reminded of how necessary and nourishing it is to bathe daily in the goodness of our Father, to be refreshed in His attributes, to be renewed with His Word. To keep one's perspective of who God is (everything!), of who I am (nothing!), of what I really deserve (hell!), and of all I've so unworthily received (Christ's righteousness!).

Friday, September 15, 2006

What a faithful God we serve and how He does meet our needs even before we have them! A van backed up to our garage yesterday with half of Costco in it! Meat for the freezer, school lunch snacks and more! Along with that, miscellaneous others continue to drop off meals and groceries and we are not lacking. As Vernon said, "the floodgates have opened." Already have a volunteer to mow lawn next week and another to bake our supply of bread.

Vernon is doing well; the nurse just left to remove the chemo bag. Unfortunately, he is filled back up again today even after his 'tap' yesterday. We were both able to attend our children's open house at school last evening. What a blessing, not only to be there, but also to be reminded of the beauty of their Christian education.

A popular song from years ago has recently been wafting through my mind. It describes winning battles, yet being wounded in the fight. It speaks of appearing strong, yet needing to retreat to His feet. Now I know that you know Who I go running to when I fall down and He does indeed pick me up.

And I also know that instead of dropping my sword, I must put on daily the full armor of God. But true it is that though you may think I am strong, it is only God's grace you see. And lately there have been many tears.

Saturday, September 16, 2006

The children had earned free tickets through a summer library reading program to a local amusement park. So today we all went as a family and had a really good day. We rented a motorized wheelchair scooter for Vernon and he said that was "just the ticket", he was comfortable, and he could have never done it without "his ride." A dear friend of mine who lives several hours away had offered to come up to help in case Vernon couldn't go along today, so that was lovely to be able to spend time with her, her husband and two children our girls' age.

I must tell you the small ways in which God shows His goodness and mercy. Just yesterday I told a friend how neat it would be if God would provide a couple of extra free tickets for Vernon and I so we wouldn't have to pay admission to the park today. Wouldn't you know I got a call saying someone had two they weren't using; could we use them? Then, tonight, on the way home from our tiring day, it was late and I was thinking about what I could put on the table quickly for supper. I knew that I had soup in the fridge and thought now wouldn't some yummy rolls go nicely with that and wondering what I could find in the freezer. Can you believe when we got home, what was awaiting us but a pan of fresh, homemade honey rolls with a note that said they would go nicely with soup. And this is just a sampling; He does this so many times, so many days. Thanks to each one of you who respond to the Spirit's prompting and are a blessing.

Vernon seems to be doing well this round of chemo. Seems we hold our breath, though, with each day's particular challenge. But we also feel like what can go wrong, armed now that we are with pills for this symptom, pills for that one, on antibiotic for this…

Last evening Vernon was able to go along with Jed to hockey practice. He said it was hard for him not to sign up for a men's league on the spot!

Looking forward to Lord's Day tomorrow. Tia just told me a bit ago that Sundays aren't fun for little girls because she can't understand the preacher. I told her that I pray for her that soon will come the day that she can truly say: "I was glad when they said unto me, let us go into the house of the Lord." (Psalms 122:1 KJV)

For your more rapid growth in grace, some of you will be cast into the furnace of affliction. Sickness, bereavement, bad conduct of children and relatives, loss of property or of reputation, may come upon you unexpectedly and press heavily on you.
In these trying circumstances, exercise patience and fortitude. Be more solicitous to have the affliction sanctified, than removed.
Glorify God while in the fire of adversity. That faith which is most tried is commonly most pure and precious.
Learn from Christ how you ought to suffer.
Let perfect submission to the will of God be aimed at.
Never indulge a murmuring or discontented spirit.
Repose with confidence on the promises.
Commit all your cares to God.
Make known your requests to Him by prayer.
Let go you're too eager grasp of the world.

Become familiar with death and the grave.
Wait patiently.

~ Archibald Alexander, 1772-1851

Sunday, September 17, 2006

Vernon writes:
Round One of Chemo was complicated by the development of cellulitis. The prescription for that was an antibiotic we named the "the wicked one" - a single but large tablet taken once a day. It was largely, we think, the cause of the difficulties we faced that week.

Round Two of Chemo took place Wednesday through Friday. By the Lord's Day we face no wild side effects. No hair loss (as if anyone would take notice in my case). No diarrhea; in fact, this time the opposite seems to be the issue. Our drug supply seems to be ready for any contingency, thanks to pharmaceuticals.

There's a song that came to mind this week after three days of drizzle, rain and cloudy skies. "There shall be showers of blessing, O that today they might fall." Yes, I agree we are showered with blessings in Christ. (In him we have redemption through his blood, the forgiveness of sins, in accordance with the riches of God's grace." ~ Ephesians 1:7 NIV) But to plead for showers seems a bit beyond my comprehension, especially when mercy drops around us are falling (why the need to be so selfish?). Mercy drops, however, I can relate to and I have fallen in love with the term: "mercy drops." God promises to grant or drop, as if behind enemy lines, mercy when needed. "Mercy drops" - sounds almost like a name for a confectionary - like a Hershey Kiss or a Starburst. Or it could almost sound like a candied medicinal product eagerly taken by ailing youngsters.

At any rate, let me tell you of some mercy drops that have fallen around us. I was seated in the waiting room on Round Two Chemo day, waiting for my call. Next to me an older lady was doing a brain teaser puzzle, the

Sudoku. My curiosity got the best of me, so she explained it all to me as she went along filling in numbers 1-9 both laterally and longitudinally, and in blocks - a tease indeed! After a bit, I mentioned that for my past-time I read theology. She did a double-take, looked at me and said, "I wish my husband was here, to talk theology with you!" She and her husband were from a PCA church in Northeast Philadelphia. 'Twas a mercy drop!

We received a designer check from friends written out to a sizable contribution. Now, some designer checks have pretty sunsets, a thought for the day, a teddy bear. This check had on it a Bible verse from Psalm 68:20 NIV. It read: "Our God is a God who saves, from the Sovereign Lord comes escape from death." Did God order that particular verse for us? Was it actually the next numbered check in line or did the sender alter the sequence to a verse deemed appropriate? We do not know but 'twas a mercy drop!

Our chemotherapy nurse for the first two treatments has been the same. She's from India and loves the Lord. Three of her brothers are missionaries in India. She has been a mercy drop.

Drizzle, rain and cloud cover tend to dampen the spirit of man as well. Who isn't affected at times? After three days of wet, rainy weather this week, Sharon was hit especially hard. One evening I was gone with the boys; upon return, I found a black binder bound with string on my nightstand. It was from Sharon. She had compiled from a website of quotes and sermon excerpts on suffering from saints in the distant past, Puritans and the like. Here is what she would call a five star sampling...

*"No discipline seems pleasant at the time,
but painful. Later on, however, it produces a
harvest of righteousness and peace for those
who have been trained by it."* ~ Hebrews 12:11 NIV

"Affliction is one of God's medicines!

*By it He often teaches lessons which
would be learned in no other way.*

*By it He often draws souls away from sin
and the world, which would otherwise have
perished everlastingly.*

*Health is a great blessing—but
sanctified disease is a greater.*

*Prosperity and worldly comfort, are what
all naturally desire—but losses and crosses
are far better for us—if they lead us to Christ.*

Let us beware of murmuring in the time of trouble.

*Let us settle it firmly in our minds, that there
is a meaning, a 'needs be', and a message from
God—in every sorrow that falls upon us.*

*There are no lessons so useful as those
learned in the school of affliction.*

*There is no commentary that opens up the
Bible so much as sickness and sorrow.*

*The resurrection morning will prove, that
many of the losses of God's people were
in reality, eternal gains.*

*Thousands at the last day, will testify with
David—'It is good for me that I have been*

afflicted!" ~ *Psalms 119:71 KJV*

~ *"One of God's medicines!" by J. C. Ryle*

'Twas a mercy drop!
This morning (Sunday) we celebrate the Lord's Supper. Remembering His death, through it we are justified and atoned. Now that's a shower of blessing - to be drenched by it we plead.

Tuesday, September 19, 2006

All is well. Vernon even mowed some lawn yesterday. And I am allowing myself the luxury of lunch out with friends this week.

Yesterday's conversation with the doctor yielded a "no" to Vernon's plea for another fluid tap. He is carrying around well over 20 pounds of fluid, which causes some extreme discomfort. But the doctor explains it is for his good to endure the misery versus taking more fluid off at this time. The reasons why are hard to explain but include risk of infection, loss of protein, and the fact that each time they drain, it just fills back up that much faster and thus is a losing battle. All we can do is pray that chemo will take effect quickly to alleviate this problem.

If you're up to another five-star sampling…

Christian reader, we suppose you to be no
stranger to grief; your heart has known what
sorrow is; you have borne, perhaps for years,
some heavy, painful, yet concealed cross.
Over it, in the solitude and silence of privacy,
you have wept, agonized, and prayed. And still
the cross, though mitigated, is not removed.

*You may be asking, 'Why, if Jesus is so
tender and sympathizing, does He place
upon me this cross?'
Because of His wisdom and love.
He sees you need that cross!
You have carried it, it may be, for years. Who
can tell where and what you would have been
at this moment, but for this very cross?
What evils in you it may have checked;
what corruptions in you it may have subdued;
what constitutional infirmities it may have weakened;
from what lengths it has kept you;
from what rocks and precipices it has guarded you;
and what good it has been silently and secretly,
yet effectually, working in you all the long years
of your life; who can tell but God Himself?
The removal of that cross might have
been the removal of your greatest mercy!
Hush, then, every murmur; be still, and know
that He is God; and that all these trials, these
sufferings, these untoward circumstances, are
now working together for your good and His glory.
And what would you know, may we not ask, of
Jesus; His tenderness, and love, and sympathizing
heart; but for the rough and thorny path along
which you have been thus led?
The glory and fullness, the preciousness and
sympathy of Christ are not learned in every
circumstance of life. The hour of prosperity,
when everything passes smoothly on:
providences smiling, the heart's surface
unruffled, the gladsome sunlight of creature*

*happiness gilding every prospect with its
brightness; this is not the hour, nor these
the circumstances, most favorable to an
experimental acquaintance with Christ.
It is in the dark hour of suffering,
the hour of trial and of adversity,
when the sea is rough,
and the sky is lowering,
and providences are mysterious,
and the heart is agitated,
and hope is disappointed,
its bud nipped, and its stem broken,
and creature comfort and support fail.
Oh, then it is the fullness, and preciousness,
and tenderness of Jesus are learned. Then
it is the heart loosens its hold on created
objects, and entwines itself more fondly
and more closely around the Incarnate
Son of God.*

~ "Some heavy, painful, yet concealed cross?" by Octavius Winslow

Wednesday, September 20, 2006

We are realizing we underestimate how much our children are ingesting of our present situation. Yesterday on the way home from school, out of the clear blue, Tia, our first grader states: "Daddy says that (a friend of ours) thinks God didn't make Daddy sick and Daddy thinks that God did but I think somewhere in the middle." Then later, in family devotions, she made the comment that she thinks God must have a problem box up in heaven and gives cancer to those that need it. Our hearts were then nourished to hear her and an older brother pray that God would help them accept what He has decided is best for us. Oh, we do not take lightly the impression we mold into our children of their Heavenly Father, yet we cannot help but live and breath our God's sovereignty and providential care.

We also continue to underestimate the hearts of God's people. It truly nourishes the soul to experience hands-on care. From hammer and nails, from mops to pails, those who come and give of themselves, I find myself desperately inadequate in expressing how this makes me feel. And truly humbling and astounding it is to me the "who" behind these givers, these pray-ers, and these do-ers. Those we know not well, those who years have distanced our paths, yet they come, they give, they care. We meekly express our gratitude. You know who you are.

And for those of you who live at a distance who frequently express your frustration about not "being here", to you I offer the following:

One of the greatest kindnesses we can do our friends, and sometimes the only kindness that is in the power of our hands, is, by prayer to recommend them to the loving kindness of God. ~ Matthew Henry

Thursday, September 21, 2006

Yesterday's doctor call resulted in two additional prescriptions for our already-lengthy roster. Vernon has now started on diuretics which is helping relieve some of the fluid pressure. "Let Jesus Christ Be Praised!"

The children and I are starting with colds and sore throats. How we pray Vernon might be spared from this added affliction.

Last night found one of our children mourning the death of his kitten. Though we might wonder why this, too, we know not how God prepares our hearts.

I see the wrong that round me lies,
I feel the guilt within;
I hear, with groan and travail cries,
The world confess its sin.

Yet, in the maddening maze of things,
And tossed by storm and flood,
To one fixed trust my spirit clings
I know that God is good!

~ John Greenleaf Whittier, 1807-1892

Saturday, September 23, 2006

Vernon continues to feel some relief with the effects of the diuretics; it has definitely helped to relieve some of the fluid pressure.

Family... those we are bonded with either by blood or law; a bond not formed by choice but cemented by necessary practice. In a time of fearful unknown, that bond becomes a sort of fierce attachment. How blessed we are to experience the presence of several of Vernon's out-of-state family this weekend: sisters from Indiana and Ohio. They've been working hard on Vernon's "Fall To-Do" list, which included much weeding and mulching, splitting wood, etc.

I wonder, sometimes, how there can be any shred of pride left in me after having messy closets and cupboards exposed to those who so kindly come to help and clean. Pride seems to have this ability to grow back as quickly as it is pruned, however. And God does continue to prune us. Pray that Vernon and I might overlook petty offenses and be forgiving of one another for times of sweet togetherness.

The weight of this sad time we must obey, speak what we feel, not what we ought to say. ~ Shakespeare

Sunday, September 24, 2006

I realize, increasingly, the value in our Lord's command of "not forsaking the assembling of ourselves together…" (Hebrews 10:25 KJV) There can be no comfort given like that of those who share in your joy (Christ!) as well as in your sorrow. How blessed we find ourselves continuously nurtured by His body. And how blessed we are each Lord's Day to be taught such scriptural truths, to worship our Maker with hymns and psalms, to fellowship together with like-minded believers.

However, as we were getting ready to go to church this morning, one of our children said he didn't feel well. Because worshiping together on the Lord's Day is the highlight of our week for both Vernon and I, we told our son to just get ready, he'd be okay. Well, as we were pulling into the church parking lot, sure enough, he vomited his discomfort and I was forced to bring him home and miss church. Through tears of disappointment, I once again wrestled and submitted to His master plan I can't begin to understand. It seems that so often lately God asks of me, "Will you believe and trust that I am truly sovereign in even this small thing?"

Monday, September 25, 2006

We earnestly solicit your prayers concerning the future of our family's income and housing. Much of the future is uncertain due to how Vernon's cancer will respond to chemo treatments. Still the desire for some sort of work for Vernon and the need for income doesn't abate. And speaking of present "income", once again, words are inadequate to describe the gratitude we feel about the gifts we have been given. To those who give through the church fund, we have no idea who you are but are overwhelmed with your generosity and sincerely thank you.

We look forward to more family coming this week. My brother and family from Michigan and also Vernon's brother from Colorado. Friday, then, will be another big day at Fox Chase with more blood work, doctor's visit, and infusion.

Thursday, September 28, 2006

It's a beautiful fall sunny morning here in the East. How good it is that God controls the weather and it does not come as a reflection of our own disposition.

Corrie Ten Boom once said: "Worry does not empty tomorrow of its sorrow, it empties today of its strength." How right she was in her echo of Jesus' command to not worry about tomorrow, for truly today does have enough trouble of its own. It is when I try to tackle more than today that the waters get deep.

Dwight L. Moody used to say there were "three kinds of faith in Jesus Christ: struggling faith, which is like a man floundering and fearful in deep water; clinging faith, which is like a man hanging to the side of the boat; and resting faith, which finds a man safe inside the boat - strong and secure enough to reach out his hand to help someone else."

My husband is a man of strong faith and of late I vacillate between borrowing from his faith or arguing him down. How difficult it is to "plan" for the future when the future is so unknown. We beg our Master for the healing of Vernon's body. Yet, more and more, I wonder if what we perceive (and plead for) as God's blessings or mercies are for our own good, actually, not blessings or mercies at all.

We eagerly look forward to our doctor's visit tomorrow. We struggle lately with wondering when and if chemo is ever going to become effective. Though the water pills have enabled Vernon's legs and feet to return to normal size, his abdomen remains incredibly uncomfortable. He has lost so much weight. Though I have witnessed his gradual decline, I still sometimes startle at his appearance. Yesterday his brother said when he first saw him (since a year ago), he hardly knew him. Yes, he eats as able (he gets full so quickly), but my brother explained that cancer feeds itself first which, apparently, isn't leaving a lot left for the rest of him.

I marvel how, at a time like this, insignificant differences become so trivial and the bond we share in Christ so vital. We are encouraged today to have family working on building deck steps for us. We are blessed beyond deservation (don't think that is a word but it should be).

Happy Storm that wrecks a man on such a rock as this!
~ Charles H. Spurgeon

Friday, September 29, 2006

We're off to Fox Chase today for blood work, doctor visit and infusion. These days tend to get a bit long. Thanks for thinking of us.

And what sacrificial friends we have! Last night I dashed off an email to a dear friend, telling her we had no one going along with us today (we thought earlier we did). When she got my e-mail at 5:30 AM, she called to say she's coming, might be just a tad late, needed to make necessary child care arrangements, etc. What a lady!

And yesterday to have three men (a brother-in-law, Vernon's brother and my brother) drop everything in their lives and put those deck steps up for us in a day's time!

Friday, September 29, 2006

Another long day, more than twelve hours away from home. So grateful were we for Fagel with her servant's heart and quiet strength.

I've come to have a new appreciation for people, created in the image of God. People we wait and wait with in the infusion room (did I mention waiting?). With some we swap stories - success or sad. With others we swap religious convictions: St. Michael, St. Catherine, etc. With still others we swap email addresses or expressions of looking forward to visiting with them again, next infusion day.

Our doctor was not discouraged with Vernon's progress. We must be patient. After one more treatment of chemo they will do another CAT scan to see what change has occurred in the liver. We are encouraged that Vernon's ascites seems lessoned, we know not from diuretics or chemo, but are thankful regardless. I must also tell you that Vernon no longer has any pain in his hip (femur) bone cancer. His primary discomfort at present is in his back, we presume to be from the abdomen pressure. So, we have much to be thankful for. Vernon may think it selfish to plead for mercy showers vs. mere drops, but God does indeed send showers in His time.

Saturday, September 30, 2006

May God bless the men from our church who gave of their time and talent this day to work on a shed roof and deck project of Vernon's. We know they have work at home of their own that awaits them, not to mention Saturday time with family sacrificed. We continue to marvel at how others bless us.

God has also been impressing on me lately how good I really have it. Yes, my husband may be dying of cancer but there are worse situations to be in. I know there are countless heartbreaking situations others experience. I am so blessed to have a husband who strives to love the Lord with all his heart, soul and strength, and who lives out his love for his wife and children. How, then, dare I complain with what God has asked me to bear? And though my husband may not live many years, we have the mercy of knowing that ahead of time and can cherish the time we have together as well as make the necessary plans we wouldn't have otherwise.

I have a much lighter heart concerning Vernon's health. His ascites has definitely lessened and he is up and about with more ease.

'Tis grace that brought me safe thus far, and it's grace that will lead me home. ~ John Newton

Wednesday, October 4, 2006

Vernon is responding well to the last bout of chemo. As they have warned, however, being very tired is the worst and main side effect. And I think we can safely say Vernon is feeling perhaps better now than he ever has in the past nearly three months. You can imagine the blessing this is.

"The people that do know their God shall be strong." ~ Daniel 11:32 KJV (Though we may not feel or understand that strength, we certainly praise Him for it!)

Thursday, October 5, 2006

When will I learn to recognize this roller coaster for what it is: an up-and-down ride with twists and turns, and when you think you're finally comfortable in your seat, you're thrown again. Okay, so there are good days and there are bad days and there are days that I don't know what to call them. But each day the Lord hath made and we valiantly try to rejoice in it.

Many folks ask about Vernon's chemo side effects. As the doctors continue to tell us, chemo has changed much in the last years and it shouldn't quite get the bad rap it does. His chemo is not likely to cause him to lose his hair. He does not experience nausea or vomiting. He does have a mouth full of sores that is common, they tell us, but it sure does not make eating enjoyable. He is very tired much of the time. This afternoon, as he lay down on the couch, he remarked that all he had gotten done today was look for a pliers. Fortunately we were able to get a chuckle out of it but it's not always a laughable matter. It's very frustrating and discouraging to not be able to do what one wants.

Grace has taken on a new meaning for us. As in the definition of undeserved goodwill. To the many who continue to show us such kindness, through sometimes a torrent of tears, we are humbled and grateful.

Friday, October 6, 2006

What follows is a portion of a letter Vernon wrote to a friend today…

We are praying for your recovery and well-being most every day. You may not see God's hand, you may feel He has abandoned you. You stand in company with the saints in the Old Testament who asked the same questions of God. Where are you? How long? David in Psalms pours out his heart to God. Jeremiah in the Lamentations cries out to God; sometimes I wonder too if my prayers are a futile exercise. Is my suffering and affliction really making me a better person? Am I a better husband because of it? Am I a better father because of it? To be honest, I would say No - I've been snappy to my wife, impatient with my kids, but God who sees the backside of the tapestry of our lives says Yes - God isn't American and his work isn't immediate gratification - He is patient, long-suffering, tender as He works in our lives slowly, but surely two steps forward, one step back conforming us to the likeness of His son. We are God's workmanship (Ephesians 2:10). On his workbench! Will God really make an inferior product out of you or me? The question is will you and I trust Him? Commit our way to Him? Believe that what He says is what He will do?

And may I say that trusting isn't mistake-free. God's best have been overcome with depression, overdosed on drugs, committed grievous sins. And we would all if not for God's restraining and pardoning grace! Hallelujah, What a Savior!

My prayer for you and I both is taken from Paul's letter to the saints in Ephesus: "I pray that the eyes of your heart may be enlightened in order that you may know the hope to which he has called you, the riches of his glorious inheritance in his holy people, and his incomparably great power for us who believe." ~ Ephesians 1:18-19 NIV

~ Vernon

Sunday, October 8, 2006

This past week held some low times, much-needed grace from above. The counsel of a friend: "Stress brings out the worst of our flesh *even while* our faith is growing." Though as we struggle with the wretchedness of ourselves in the midst of this trial, we are yet encouraged that, though it be beyond our comprehension, sanctification might continue.

We continue to have hope that the cancer is under attack in Vernon's body; the swelling in his abdomen significantly decreased. His weight loss is a current concern.

Some talk of Santa's elves and the work they accomplish: we talk of God's own - those who came again this week wielding hammer and saw. One of Vernon's sisters and her family have spent many an hour working into the dark, cold hours of the evening on a fence project by the tree house. And more work done on the barn by church men. Though, of course, Vernon's first choice would've been to do this work himself, what better second than to have each nail secured with the love of God in flesh?

This Lord's Day will forever hold a special place in our memory as we participated in the baptism of our children; the three eldest as professions of faith, the youngest as a covenant child. How meaningful to share this precious milestone with family and friends.

Wednesday, October 11, 2006

Yesterday was a fairly uneventful day (that's good!). Vernon's sister Kathy was our accompaniment and chauffeur - always a blessing. She read to us some portions of a book on Grace by Jerry Bridges while we passed the time watching the drips in the infusion room. More and more I marvel at God's grace and our unworthiness of it. We didn't actually have a doctor appointment but did run into our doctor in the café so that was neat. He was encouraged with Vernon's condition and even said he could start cutting back on some of his meds and see how he does. Vernon's blood counts were good. We go for a CAT scan of the liver next week.

Again, not sure we fully recognize how a Daddy who isn't well affects our little ones and consumes their world more than we realize. Our six-year old wrote in her journal a few days ago: "I would like if u would get my dad better." And nearly every night in bedtime prayers, after praying for Daddy to "get better," she adds this phrase in almost a breathless whisper: "Do what you think is best." It's heart-wrenching and comforting all at once - this raw faith of a little child.

Lord willing, we will leave for Ohio for one of Vernon's nephew's wedding this weekend. We may leave as soon as he gets his chemo bag unhooked tomorrow afternoon so we could split up the trip and stop overnight, or we may just leave Friday morning. We welcome prayers for traveling mercies and Vernon's health and comfort throughout the weekend. Fall is Vernon's favorite season so the colorful leaves along the way should serve as a majestic reminder of our Creator.

Monday, October 16, 2006

Thank you for your prayers for traveling mercies for our trip to Ohio. Vernon's biggest hardship was dealing with the children's exuberance. He even drove half the way coming and returning home. We've heard many encouraging comments about his improved appearance above several weeks ago. "Let Jesus Christ Be Praised!"

Memories of the weekend include…

Time with family… those who know you best but love you still, whose earnest hugs speak volumes only the heart can hear. We are blessed!

Time with old friends… a bond of long years known. Thank you for hospitality shown.

Time with new friends… we were able to put more than a face to names we've known; another couple our age also with four children of similar ages to ours. He, too, faced with a grim cancer prognosis. We shared, we compared, we laughed, we cried, we prayed. We joked about how we know the medical and cancer lingo now; words just months ago we knew not their meaning, now their meaning all too clear. We sat in their living room and these two men poured out their hearts to God, men who can no longer play football with their boys, men who may not live to usher these same boys into manhood, yet men who say of God, "Thou art good", and do not doubt that "He doeth all things well." Surely the presence of the Lord was in that place.

We shared in the joy of the union of Vernon's nephew in marriage to his bride, also the engagement of a dear friend of mine. What a blessing this institute of marriage God designed. We were encouraged by the exuberance of young love. Love not yet stood the test of time nor had those vows challenged. God's grace on the journey to these two couples basking in their love and His.

We worshiped together with the believers at Haven. We marvel at the fellowship of the saints; those we know not well, or not at all, yet they share in our suffering. Our bond in Christ 'twines our hearts together. My heart aches for those who share not in the comfort of Christ's love and the fellowship of His body. Blest be indeed the tie that binds, we can attest to others oft flowing the sympathizing tear.

Wednesday, October 18, 2006

Another five star sampling...

"I have refined you in the furnace of suffering." ~ Isaiah 48:10

A sculptor does not use a 'manicure set' to reduce the crude, unshapely marble to a thing of beauty. The saw, the hammer and the chisel are cruel tools, but without them the rough stone must remain forever formless and unbeautiful.

To do His supreme work of grace within you, God will take from your heart everything you love most. Everything you trust in will go from you. Piles of ashes will lie where your most precious treasures used to be!

~ "Cruel Tools" by A. W. Tozer

Thursday, October 19, 2006

Yesterday we picked up my cousin Rose from Chicago at the Philadelphia airport who has come to help out the next ten days. What a blessing to have an in-house cook, childcare provider and chauffeur.

Today Vernon is going with Tia on a local museum field trip. After mentioning it to her yesterday that he might go along, there was no backing out for his soft Daddy's heart upon seeing her joy and excitement.

Tomorrow we go down to Fox Chase Cancer Center for a routine CAT scan done after the first four rounds of chemo to compare with the baseline scan and see what effect has been made. We are both excited and anxious about the results (which we will not find out until next week).

These Clouds We So Much Dread

Saturday, October 21, 2006

This day finds Vernon a bit nostalgic. Years back, he combined his love for the fall foliage with his passion for golf in establishing an annual golf day with a group of friends. Today they golf without him.

At times I find myself in a quandary, attempting to write an honest journal entry while preserving the dignity of loved ones. One must, I suppose, retain some sense of propriety even in baring one's soul, though those who know me well could attest to brutal honesty being one of my besetting sins. A question I hear often is how might one best pray for us? I am most grateful that we have a high priest who intercedes for us between the Father when our tears and groans cannot express in words what we desire to implore. Day-by-day settling into this new way of life yet unknown, an uncertainty of the future yet unknown, doesn't come naturally. I vacillate between hopefulness for the future and hopelessness in the present. Though we deny not His goodness nor His grace, yet still we face this fluctuating maze.

In some ways I mourn the life we used to know. We are not immune to the poisons of the evil one. We so earnestly desire to have the fruits of The Spirit manifested in our everyday lives and interaction with each other in our family. But stress and pain do not naturally invite gentleness and selflessness. And though each day may bring new privileges and you see a smile on our face, tears hover just beneath the surface and our composure not unlike a child's precarious seashore castle moat. So many kind folks ask: "How are you?" and even as the words leave their mouth, we sense our discomfort realizing the ridiculous of the question. Out of the internet's top 58 results for the definition of "good," I found a few that enable me to continue to answer the question truthfully. Of course never forgetting that *God is good and we are God's.*

Simon, Simon, behold, Satan demanded to have you, that he might sift you like wheat, but I have prayed for you that your faith may not fail. And when you have turned again, strengthen your brothers. ~ Luke 22:31-32 ESV

Steadfastness in believing doth not exclude all temptations from without. When we say a tree is firmly rooted, we do not say the wind never blows upon it. ~ John Owen, 1616-1683

Tuesday, October 24, 2006

O Lord, who didst illumine the heart of Thomas with the clear radiance of Thy risen glory, Thou knowest how to deal with the doubts and perplexities of my heart. I have not seen; give me the blessedness of those who have believed. ~ F.B. Meyer, 1847-1929

Thursday, October 26, 2006

A "Let Jesus Christ Be Praised" Report…

I fear I've become negligent in sharing encouraging news. Within the last few weeks, Vernon has graduated from sleeping on the couch to on his back in bed for the first time since surgery. Also, one day this week he was pleased to announce that he had his work boots on for the first time since early July. And this past week has found him doing some woodworking in the garage and even some fall landscaping maintenance at a job. We think, too, he is gaining some of his weight back (not fluid weight) as he doesn't look quite so gaunt. And we are in the process of weaning him off both his water pills and pain pills.

Whew! "Let Jesus Christ Be Praised," indeed! My heart leaps sometimes at the thought of God possibly miraculously healing him completely of this dreadful cancer.

Another huge relief is a phone call I had yesterday with our medical sharing plan which looks like they will be covering our medical expenses. Feels like a load looming overhead has been lifted. It is not in writing yet but the report was positive.

Tomorrow will find us at Fox Chase for another long day. Blood work, doctor visit (find out CAT scan reading) and infusion.

Thanks for continuing in intercession with us.

I praise you Alpha and Omega,
God at the beginning
God at the end
Always God.

~ Mary Morrison Suggs

Friday, October 27, 2006

I type what Vernon shares tonight:

"Ah! Wither could I go for aid when
tempted, desolate, dismayed
Or how the hosts of hell defeat
had suffering saints no mercy seat!"

~ Thomas Hastings, 1784-1872

Oh, one could say you've not suffered much.
The past week's news have been relatively news free.

No news is good news - the adage tells.
Your complexion is better - your face filled out.
You're doing some work - you're out and about.
The cat scan must validate the same to be sure.

But things are never sure with cancer.
Friday was more trick and no treat.
The doctor says the cat scan has shown
the spots on the liver have slightly grown.
You may also need a pin in your bone.
A new chemo treatment - side effects unknown
The creatures we are - we let out a groan
The Creator it seems has a mind of His own!

"Who has known the mind of the Lord,
Or who has been His counselor?" (Romans 11:34 NIV)
Yes, the scriptures do bear witness
to the fact - He's free to think,
and free to act - that from
him, and through Him,
and to Him are all things.
To Him be the glory forever. Amen

The apostle also writes, we read this morning from Spurgeon, of *"four faithful sayings."* One of which (found in II Timothy 2:12 KJV) gave us great comfort as the day's events played out. The faithful saying is: *"If we suffer, we shall also reign with Him."* What a God: to make from clay and cancer co-regents with Him, both now and for all eternity.

What follows now are my disjointed musings on the day…

We are fallen creatures indeed. The words Vernon uttered when the doctor left the room this morning our Brother James forbids me from printing. And I must confess that there are times I look around the infusion room at mostly older folks and stifle feelings of resentment. There was a time I had to lock myself in the bathroom today and simply sob.

We can only clench our fists in frustration, shake our heads in wonder, let the tears flow, and rest in God's total sovereignty once again.

Brother James also admonishes us to "Consider it pure joy, my brothers and sisters, whenever you face trials of many kinds…" (James 1:2 NIV) I can only conclude that that joy is most definitely not the one that first comes to mind. That joy has to be a sense of security in our Savior vs. an exuberance in our present situation.

Is it possible to be discouraged without being disheartened? I believe so. Then again, ask me tomorrow and my answer may differ. But by God's grace I will continue to proclaim He is able, He is faithful, and He is good.

We are puzzled, we are perplexed. Cancer, with its many tentacles of confusion, grips us again. The doctors have no valid explanation for our report today save that cancer defies "sense".

In so many ways Vernon is better; he looks significantly better than a few weeks ago, his stomach is down, has less pain. So we had little apprehension of the CAT scan results being negative.

However, the doctor was disappointed to find the golf-ball sized tumors in the liver had actually grown since chemo, and not shrunk as was the goal. What this means is that chemo thus far has been basically ineffective. Quite a blow, yes. The doctor remains optimistic, however, with Vernon's general good health and other treatment options available if this next one proves to be ineffective as well. Today they started a new drug called

Irinotecan (Vernon, ever full of dry humor, inquired of the doctor whether it came in a tin can). This will be administered on a three-week schedule and he no longer needs to carry the bag for two days. This is good news for Vernon. His bag buddy was enough to nearly bring him to tears. This new drug's main possible side effects include diarrhea, fatigue and low white blood cell counts, nausea, and possible loss of hair. After six weeks, they will do another CAT scan to determine the effectiveness of this drug. If his body doesn't respond positively to this one, either, there are several more drugs they can try.

Another issue now: near Vernon's incision on his stomach there seems to be a tender, distended area that is becoming more noticeable. The doctor today said he thinks most likely what happened was during the surgery the cancer cells that were "loose" attached to the bowel and the wall of the abdomen near the incision. Sigh.

His weight was down a bit more today, which also surprised us as his face seems to be filling out.

He will need to continue on the water pills as needed.

Next Friday we have an MRI scheduled on his femur and pelvis. He does experience discomfort in his hip when he walks. They explained the cancer is where the femur makes an angle. There is cancer in both the hip and the femur. After the MRI, we will see a bone surgeon to determine whether it is necessary to have a rod put in to strengthen the bone to prevent a fracture, or if radiation will be sufficient. Please, please pray that surgery will not be necessary. Another surgery and hospital stay is almost more than Vernon can bear to think of. Meanwhile he is to continue to exercise some caution to avoid a fracture.

Please pray with us as Vernon continues to desire some sort of income providing labor he would be able to do while facing these physical limitations and the uncertainty of the future.

We have the most interesting conversations with our friends (fellow patients and their spouses) down at the cancer center. Some Evangelicals, some Catholics, some Jewish. One today openly admitting to being very angry at God. Most cling to Him and express commitment to prayer. Honesty isn't optional. Some sort of casually brush it off; one elderly couple said today, "Ah well, we're old anyway." Everyone understands. Taking one day at a time seems to be the popular mode of survival. Everyone has this sense of "loom of gloom" over them; we are just in different stages of experiencing it. As you compare your diagnosis and where you are at with it and with God, there is an indescribable bond. Something that struck me today is that for the amount of people who don't believe that suffering comes from God, why then do they bother to get upset with Him? Do we just blame Him when it is convenient? I think many are afraid to admit He is in control as the idea that He is in control and can still be good, despite our pain and confusion, is incomprehensible. God help us all. Numerous times I must remind myself God needs no defense lawyer. He can handle His own reputation.

Selfishness defiles our tears, and unbelief tampers with our faith.
~ C. H. Spurgeon

Sunday, October 29, 2006

Vernon's body seems to be tolerating the new chemo drug well as far as negative side effects go. "Let Jesus Christ Be Praised."

Whatever the cost to us in loss of friends or goods or length of days - let us know Thee as Thou art, that we may adore Thee as we should.
~ A. W. Tozer

These Clouds We So Much Dread

Tuesday, October 31, 2006

Vernon is back on water pills and pain pills, his abdomen the culprit. Though today found him out trimming his mother's shrubs.

Vernon's MRI's of the hip and pelvis are rescheduled for the second week in November. The plan is to see the bone surgeon that afternoon to go over them.

Saturday, November 4, 2006

Sometimes I think that we should have two websites. One for those who come to check on how Vernon is doing (I can tell you somewhat how he is doing health-wise, but not otherwise). And then one for my friends who want to know how I am doing (and not health-wise). I do find myself intimidated by the broad audience and will warn those reading now that what follows is my mere musings. The silence or lack of posts of late is not entirely due to time restrictions. The balance between saying what one wishes they could say and the truth of what is actually felt is not a fine line in my mind. So if you're expecting to read theological correctness and sugar cubes of inspiration, you'll need to look elsewhere. Am I wallowing in despair? Am I treading in a cesspool of self-pity? I think not. Did not our Saviour in the garden sweat drops of blood as he begged for the cup to be passed from Him? I submit to my Heavenly Father's plan, but it does not mean I don't writhe and weep during the battle.

I am tired. I am really tired. I am tired of life as it now consists. Tired of each day seeming like a puzzle piece that we don't have the cover on the box for. Tired of a frustrated husband who cannot work. Tired of living off of other people.

Tired of being strong. Tired of children who are hurting. Tired of trying to understand sanctification in the midst of my rottenness. The other day as Vernon was reading aloud to me about how trials are such a blessing, I said, "Okay, can it be someone else's turn to get 'blessed' now?!" And the other night when Vernon made the comment about his cancer being good for him, Tia insisted that it just simply *could not* be good for him. I assured her it is not something we are necessarily able to understand, but trust our God we must.

I dislike fall. I never did like the season because it is the forerunner to the coldest time of year that, for me, equates misery. Then, when my beloved Mother died five years ago in November, my distaste for the season was intensified. Dead and barrenness everywhere you look outside. Now my father has chosen to remarry in the same season.

An acquaintance of ours died from a brain tumor a few days ago. She also happened to be the grandma to one of our children's classmates. When my son asked me why she died, I opened my mouth to say the word "cancer" and stopped myself just in time. It can be a tightrope we walk: being honest, yet protective with the children.

However, I am blessed. I am blessed first and foremost by God's grace that is increasingly beyond my comprehension. That Christ's righteousness covers my heinousness is inexpressibly amazing. I am blessed with the sun on these crisp, fall days that takes the bite out of the chill. I am blessed with four precious children who make getting up each day a joy. I am blessed with a honey-haired doll who brings distraction to my days while the others are in school. I am blessed with the satisfaction that only an early morning cup of coffee can bring. I am blessed with a dog whose uncontrollable affection is somehow nourishing. I am blessed that Vernon's health enabled us to enjoy a day together yesterday as a family at the Baltimore Aquarium. I am blessed to have shared a special tea time today with my oldest princess. I am blessed with the Word of God that brings perspective to my hurting heart and parched soul. I am blessed with friends and family who care and continue to show that concern in tangible ways. I am blessed by the reminder in ladies' Bible Study this morning that "it is not the strength of our faith that saves us." Praise God, what a blessing indeed!

A man can no more take in a supply of grace for the future than he can eat enough for the next six months, or take sufficient air into his lungs at one time to sustain life for a week. We must draw upon God's boundless store of grace from day to day as need it. ~ D. L. Moody

Monday, November 06, 2006

My cousin Rose wrote the following in her journal after she flew home last week...

Just returned from Sharon's last night -
the pain, the despair, the frantic whirl of normalizing activity,
pushing fatigue to exhaustion, tension to anger,
and mixing tears with relieving laughter.
It's a bow strung too tight, yet the daily tunes are continually played upon it,
rending melodies of piercing intensity - wrought with love, hope and utter despair,
shrill and loud, they carry on the will to live, to sustain - perhaps the man, perhaps the memory of him.
In hymns, lullabies and endless lessons, songs fall upon upon small ears reaching them, teaching them and finally
beseeching them to pick up the tune, carry their part,
and continue the bittersweet song when their parents cannot.

Tuesday, November 7, 2006

The sorest afflictions never appear intolerable, but when we see them in the wrong light: when we see them in the hand of God, Who dispenses them; when we know that it is our loving Father who abases and distresses us; our sufferings will lose their bitterness and become even a matter of consolation.
~ Brother Lawrence, 1605-1691

Wednesday November 8, 2006

Well, tomorrow promises to be another long day at Fox Chase. Vernon's MRI's begin at 9:00; kindly pray for him. He is naturally apprehensive about them as we have all heard horror stories of the claustrophobic conditions. He is to have two of them: one for the hip and one for the pelvis. Each, I was told, about forty-five minutes long. We then have an appointment with the bone surgeon at 3:00 and he will go over the results with us and give his recommendation (surgery for a pin to strengthen the femur or radiation). I am scared. So many times we have received worse news than anticipated.

I bless Thee, O most holy God… that I, a weak and erring mortal, should have this ready access to the heart of Him who moves the stars.
~ John Baillie, 1886-1960

Thursday, November 9, 2006

The MRI's went well today - thanks to those of you who were remembering Vernon in prayer over that time. He said it really wasn't that bad of an experience; not the coffin-like claustrophobic condition we had imagined.

In our waiting time between MRI's and our doctor appointment today, we drove to Penn's Landing, somewhere Vernon had always wanted to go. We strolled along the Delaware River hand in hand, sun shining, pigeons soliciting - time was bittersweet.

As one cancer veteran we met today expressed it: "When you have cancer, you must live today. Tomorrow is a long way off."

"God have mercy" was a prayer oft breathed as today's appointment approached. So, I cannot adequately express the heaviness that descended in my heart as the surgeons proceeded to tell us what we did not want to hear.

The team of four specialists who looked at Vernon's MRI's were alarmed with what they saw and expressed it as "quite impressive." The cancer is extensively from the neck of the femur (hip joint) and down midway to the knee. They are insisting upon surgery, as soon as possible, to insert a rod the entire length of the femur with a screw in each end. They said the risk of Vernon breaking his femur at this point on a scale of one to ten would be an eight. They want him to begin using crutches immediately to keep weight off the fragile bone (could it be his weight loss has been a blessing in disguise?). They regaled us with horror stories of what happens without this preventive surgery. The surgery needs to be done at a hospital with a special kind of expensive table (Lankenau Hospital). The surgery itself should take no more than forty-five minutes with only an overnight hospital stay (now that's not such bad news!). He would have one approximately four-inch incision and two more two-inch incisions for the screws. He could begin walking on it the next day. They feel the surgery important enough to interrupt his chemo regimen. They would still do radiation on the bone afterward.

Sigh. Though my husband tells me I am pitying myself when I get this way, I must confess I want to bawl. I want to crawl in a hole and not come out. I don't want him to have to go through another surgery. I don't want my children to be scared. So, what am I saying? I want life to be normal and peaceful? When will I wake up? I know the path ahead isn't the scenic route. But I know the God who maps the terrain.

Those of you who know my husband well know he is a stubborn man. The doctor admitted today that his stubbornness and high threshold of pain tolerance has gotten him far in this battle. All that to say, Vernon still isn't convinced surgery is crucial at this point and isn't committing to crutches either. May God give us wisdom and patience.

Not until then (when things we depend on are taken away) will our souls learn to rejoice in the Lord only, and to joy in the God of our salvation.
~ Hannah Whitall Smith

Friday, November 10, 2006

Sometimes life moves way too fast. Surgery is scheduled for Tuesday in Philadelphia. We do not know details yet, as they are adding him onto the schedule because they feel it is crucial to get this rod in before a break in the bone occurs.

Sunday, November 12, 2006

Vernon is scheduled for pre-admission testing tomorrow morning at 7:30 (blood work, EKG, chest x-ray - all standard procedures prior to surgery). We should find out then what time to expect surgery on Tuesday.

Please pray for our children the next three days as they experience being shuffled about as well as concern for their

Daddy. Pray for Vernon to have peace concerning all aspects of the surgery and hospital stay.

Monday, November 13, 2006

We are to report for surgery prep tomorrow at 1:00. They couldn't give an actual time for surgery. I plan on staying in overnight with him. Unless I can find some internet access somewhere, I won't be able to update till Wednesday evening when we hopefully return home.
So grateful for all your prayers.

Wednesday, November 15, 2006

Guest entry on behalf of Sharon and Vernon (for the sake of all of you who are logging on expecting to hear that Vernon is back home):
Sharon and Vernon will be at Lankenau Hospital again tonight. Apparently, the surgeon downplayed the procedure a bit and forgot to mention the need for Vernon to be on blood thinners (to prevent clots) and strong pain meds for the first couple of days. Other than some significant pain, Vernon is doing well and hoping (and would appreciate your prayers to that end) that he can come home tomorrow. As always, they are grateful for your prayers, love and interest. Hopefully, Sharon will be able to give you a more complete update on Thursday when they get settled back home.

Thursday, November 16, 2006

It seems the medical profession is under no obligation to uphold the courtroom oath of telling "the truth, the whole truth and nothing but the truth." Rather, they dispense portions of the truth merely at their discretion. Though, in retrospect, Vernon is grateful he did not know all we know now prior to surgery or it would have been more difficult for him going into it. Surgery was more of an ordeal than they originally made it sound, recovery definitely more painful and time consuming than previously explained. But here we are complete with walker, crutches, pain meds, and home health care to do physical therapy. We are grateful the surgery went well, and we are home and so glad of it! While in the hospital, he was treated like a real VIP; all sorts of medical personnel coming through our door to address this issue or that. The staff at Lankenau was wonderful and God even granted us a private room so I was able to stay in both nights with Vernon. Blood clots will be an issue of concern for a few months. Cancer in itself puts one at risk for that and bone surgery (especially when it involves the hip) increases the likelihood.

While in the hospital this time, the following hymn was the one most often sang for words of powerfully comfort...

How firm a foundation, ye saints of the Lord,
is laid for your faith in his excellent word!
What more can he say than to you he hath said,
to you that for refuge to Jesus have fled?

Fear not, I am with thee; O be not dismayed!
For I am thy God, and will still give thee aid;
I'll strengthen thee, help thee, and cause thee to stand,
upheld by my righteous, omnipotent hand.

When through the deep waters I call thee to go,
the rivers of woe shall not thee overflow;

for I will be with thee, thy troubles to bless,
and sanctify to thee thy deepest distress.

When through fiery trials thy pathway shall lie,
my grace, all sufficient, shall be thy supply;
the flame shall not hurt thee; I only design
thy dross to consume, and thy gold to refine.

The soul that on Jesus hath leaned for repose,
I will not, I will not desert to its foes;
that soul, though all hell shall endeavor to shake,
I'll never, no, never, no, never forsake.

~ "How Firm a Foundation" by John Rippon, 1787

Friday, November 17, 2006

Vernon is still experiencing considerable pain, though definitely lessened from yesterday. I am so thankful that today we were both able to attend a school program for Tia that she really wanted her Daddy there for. We borrowed a wheelchair.

Timely encouraged and challenged by these words tonight:

Depend upon it, where self begins sorrow begins;
but if God be my supreme delight and only object,
To me 'tis equal whether love ordain
My life or death - appoint me ease or pain.

~ C. H. Spurgeon

No matter how painful the pruning, God did design the rose.

Saturday, November 18, 2006

Vernon is losing his hair! He is encouraged as he takes this to mean his last bout of chemo is being effective. We feel it unfortunate that this surgery is causing him to miss a round.

Every day brings less pain and increased mobility, though crutches and pain meds are still his constant companions. And he is back to sleeping on the couch.

'Tis Jesus, the first and the last,
Whose Spirit shall guide us safe home;
We'll praise Him for all that is past,
And trust Him for all that's to come.

~ Joseph Hart, 1712-1768

Tuesday, November 21, 2006

Hooray, no physical therapy! They called to schedule an appointment for Sunday morning and when I said we wouldn't be here, we would be at church, the guy exclaimed: "What, he's going to church?!" The therapist did come out that afternoon then, but decided that with as mobile as Vernon is, he didn't need help. He just gave him some exercises to do. We meet with the surgeon next Monday to have stitches removed and to receive further recovery instructions. Meanwhile he is to stay on both crutches.

We love the prayers of children and are encouraged by those who share them with us. One of Vernon's sisters told of how his niece prayed last night "that God would heal Vernie as fast as He can." Our children's repetitive prayer is that God "would get Daddy better."

What strikes me of late is that if ever there were a case for proof that God does not "reward" according to "merit", it is being displayed in our situation. My husband and I are so incredibly unworthy of God's goodness that He continuously and monumentally heaps upon us. It is simply overwhelming. I wonder if our finite minds can ever begin to comprehend the grace of God with its multiple tentacles of pure goodness and mercy. "Glory Be His Name" seems so small a tribute, yet all we can offer.

I need never wonder where our next meal is coming from. I am constantly turning down help. When I pump gas or buy milk, I am reminded it is by the gifts of God's people that I am able to do so. May I thank those of you again who fulfill Romans 12 by "sharing with God's people who are in need."

Lord willing, we fly next Tuesday to Florida for my father's wedding. We will be gone a week. The trip obviously a matter worthy of prayer with Vernon's condition.

Thursday, November 23, 2006

We went and had family photos taken yesterday (the first in eight years - my husband not being fond of picture taking). I was going to wait for his face to fill out a bit more (yes, faith) but now that he is losing his hair... ya can't win for losing in this game.

Truly, living with this present "disability" situation is hard to get used to for all of us. The children took turns pushing the wheelchair (Vernon needs to bear with his inexperienced drivers) and we all need to slow our pace down for the crutches. You really find out which stores/aisles/curbs/buildings etc. are accessible.

Came across this recently and it struck me both with conviction and humor:

I am often, I believe, praying for others
when I should be doing things for them.
It's so much easier to pray for a bore
than to go and see him.

~ C.S. Lewis

(so that explains it, smile)

Our appointment with the bone surgeon on Monday needed to be rescheduled (the doctor is probably going hunting!) to have the stitches removed and further recovery instructions given. Because we leave for Florida on Tuesday, we can't get in till the Wednesday after we get back a week later. So, now Vernon must remain on crutches the entire trip. I really struggled with disappointment and frustration at this roadblock. I mentioned to Vernon, though, that if one truly comprehended the complete Sovereignty of God, how could there be room for discouragement in the believer's life? He reminded me that, alas, we are mere mortals.

We spent Thanksgiving Day with Vernon's family, reminded how grateful we are for family.

Saturday, November 25, 2006

His daily mercies to us are all sweetened with
this reflection- that we are saved souls.

Our morsel may be dry, but we dip it in
this dainty sauce of his salvation.

It is true I am poor, but I am saved.

These Clouds We So Much Dread

It is true I am sick, but I am saved.

*It is true I am obscure and unknown, but I am saved;
and the salvation of God sweetens all.*

*He that can grasp the salvation which is in Christ and say,
'This is mine,' is rich to all the intents of bliss, and has
his daily life gilded with joy.*

~ "Daily Blessings for God's People" by C.H. Spurgeon

Monday, November 27, 2006

Vernon's parents are driving us to the airport tomorrow morning, leaving home here at 5 AM. Thankfully we have a non-stop flight and we can take advantage of all the handicap services the airport has to offer. The children are so very excited.

I plan to be in touch on the trip; I am sure I can find internet connection somewhere.

C. H. Spurgeon once said something to the effect that those who are in the habit of thanking God for His mercies will never lack for a mercy for which to thank Him.

Tuesday, November 28, 2006

To all you dear people who keep close tabs on us:

We are in Florida safe and sound in mind and soul. We had an excellent trip. Vernon had some trouble at the security checkpoint; the surgeon had told us that the rod shouldn't give him trouble as it is titanium, but something sure did. We expected perhaps the metal staples that are still in would be a problem but actually their wand kept beeping down further on his leg - a screw perhaps? They finally just gave up on him. Vernon didn't think he looked like a criminal "all gaunt and sick" (his words, not mine).

Some of you fellow cheapskates will appreciate the scene I can only attempt to describe for you of the children and I lugging all our stuff through the airport with Vernon hobbling along on his crutches, regardless of the fact that there are carts to rent and sky caps in need of work. So, we had weary girls and boys with luggage skiing on its side, etc. - hey, perhaps we lightened someone's day with the absurdity of it all.

It sure was fun to see the children enjoying the flight. None of them remember flying and it has been six years since we've been to Florida so most don't remember Florida, either. Their excitement is enjoyable; wish their energy would be contagious as well. My cousin Rose from Chicago flew into the Tampa airport just minutes before us so we have our "nanny" again. The temperature was gorgeous today - nearly 80 degrees.

Sunday, December 3, 2006

Well, finding internet access was not as simple as I previously thought. Answers to some commonly-thought questions about how our Florida Trip is going thus far:

My Father's Wedding: I was not prepared for the torrent of emotion that accompanied the events of the day. Memories of my mother powerful and painful. Though I rejoice with my father in his bride and the companionship she provides, to say it was a difficult day would be an understatement.

Family: The bond we share not always one we'd choose but a bond we seem to cling to with fierce determination; stress and family bonding doing a delicate dance.

Vernon's Health: God once again answering many prayers with His characteristic Goodness and Mercy. Vernon is faring very well, even went along to the beach several days and on a short hike at a park as well. We rented an electric three-wheeled bike for him to cruise Pinecraft with, too.

Weather: Lovely; I don't want to go home!

I believe the children are all tucking away fond memories of this vacation.

Tuesday, December 5, 2006

As we all know, there is truly no place like home. Though hard it was to leave the balmy weather and relaxed schedule of Florida and step into frigid Pennsylvania in December and the rat race of battling cancer again, we are grateful for the many, many mercies our Heavenly Father bestowed upon us the past week.

We are heavy in hearts tonight, though, as we received sorrowful news even before we had our bags in the door. Yesterday our 81-year old neighbor and a dear friend of ours, fell off of a ladder from about twenty feet onto the pavement. He has multiple broken bones and a fractured skull. He lies in intensive care and we covet your prayers on his behalf.

Tomorrow promises to be a taxing day. Not only do we have our typically full chemo day but also have an appointment with the bone surgeon to have the staples removed, etc. (which is at another location in Philly). Thanks for remembering our children on these days as well. They do not particularly appreciate having to be cared for by others both before and after school. Kezia usually spends the day with Grandma.

Devotion is the real spiritual sweetness which takes away all bitterness from mortifications, and prevents consolations from disagreeing with the soul;

it cures the poor of sadness, and the rich of presumption; it keeps the oppressed from feeling desolate, and the prosperous from insolence; it averts sadness from the lonely, and dissipation from social life; it is as warmth in winter and as refreshing dew in summer; it knows how to abound and how to suffer want, how to profit alike by honor and by contempt; it accepts gladness and sadness with an even mind, and fills men's hearts with a wondrous sweetness. ~ Francois de Sales, 1567-1622

Wednesday, December 6, 2006

Indeed it was a long day: eleven hours away from home. So grateful for those who help with childcare, school carpooling, etc.

The staples are out, the bone surgeon says Vernon is doing great, can start using a cane instead of crutches and should start radiation for the femur as soon as possible.

Tomorrow we look into finding a radiation oncologist that our health-sharing plan will cover. Since radiation will be a daily thing for some weeks, it would be nicer to find something closer than Philadelphia.

Started the second round of this new chemo today, praying for lack of negative side effects. Our oncologist said that due to the disruption in the schedule (because of surgery) the next CAT scan may not be entirely accurate as to the effectiveness of the current drug they are using, so he expects we will continue to use this for the next six to nine weeks, and then reevaluate. He spoke soberly today of Vernon's condition. I don't need to tell you this is hard for us each one, both boys wept tonight as their Daddy spoke freely with them that this may be his last Christmas with us. We covet prayers in how much to share with our children and wisdom as we laugh, cry and pray together. We don't want to overreact.

We remember in my mother's case as she battled her cancer, she found it hard to be honest about the reality of her condition and was adamant that she was going to be healed. Talking about death and her not being here wasn't acceptable to her and that was difficult for us as family. We don't wish to shelter our children nor, however, overburden them with more than their little hearts can take.

In many ways Vernon feels better and looks better than he once did. But we still have reservations about what might be happening on the inside of his body. In an attempt to explain this, I will share cautiously that Vernon is taking an alternative supplement in massive doses that we believe God may be using to improve his health and perhaps lead to greater and further healing. However God chooses to work, we attempt to praise Him remembering He is indeed faithful, able and good.

Met a married couple today in the infusion room and both of them were cancer patients, receiving treatment there! Though I'd like to think that there is always someone worse off than oneself, I can't help but also think that they are an older couple and don't have four dear little people yet at home in need of their Daddy.

My faith does not rest on what I am or will be or will feel or will know, but in what Christ is, in what he has done, and in what he is now doing for me. ~ C. H. Spurgeon

Saturday, December 9, 2006

This latest round of chemo mainly manifested itself in causing Vernon to be very tired.

A local church that is putting on a live nativity has delegated the donations to bless us. We are humbly grateful.

The brevity of life brought close to home today. One of my best friend's father died suddenly last night from what they expect of a heart attack. How blessed it is to "mourn with those who mourn."

Our neighbor, Carl, is out of ICU but has a long road ahead of him due to the extent of his injuries. He was a frequent visitor to our home the past five months since Vernon hasn't been able to work and they spent many hours together. The rehabilitation he faces will never enable him to live as our neighbor again. How we miss him already.

We have an appointment with a radiation oncologist next Thursday in Exton which, thankfully, is only a half hour from home. Do pray for wisdom in treatment options.

I am convinced that none of us have appreciated how deeply it wounds the loving heart of our Lord, when He finds that His people do not feel safe in His care. ~ Hannah Whitall Smith

Wednesday, December 13, 2006

Attending a funeral with the memory of a past loss still tender and a likely loss to come prevalent on my heart could prove to be a quite disheartening experience. I pled for mercy in advance and once again the mercy drops fell. Though I cannot help but shudder at what is likely God will yet ask me to bear, today once again there was great evidence in the family of my friend of the evidence of God's grace. I was awed by the widow who sat in the front row and smiled nearly the entire funeral. And what a security of hope in heaven we have. Thomas Brooks wrote that "a Christian knows that death shall bring him to a more clear, full, perfect, and constant enjoyment of God! This makes him sweetly and triumphantly to sing it out, 'O death! where is your sting? O grave! where is your victory?'" (1 Corinthians 15:55 KJV)

Oh that it wouldn't take the loss or impending loss of a loved one to strengthen our relationships, or that we wouldn't need to be faced with pain and grief to cause us to nurture and value what we have. Oh that it wouldn't take the heart-wrenching nausea of grief to bring us our knees in absolute humility and dependency before our Father; to cause us to commune with Him in an intimacy never before experienced. That it wouldn't take a life altering circumstance to cause us as brothers and sisters in our Lord Jesus Christ to "encourage one another daily." (Hebrews 3:13 NIV)

Not that many years ago, I couldn't have given you a definition of the word "grace". Now it seems to define my very existence. Standing alongside my friend and her family in their sudden, unexpected loss of their loved one, I feel like I've also been in a front-row seat of witnessing God's sustaining grace to His own and also through sending those "with skin on": His church, the community of believers networked literally across the nations. Prayers and tangible expressions of our mutual Father's love binds our hearts in ways never imagined. Currently walking through a very low tide with a neighbor who isn't blessed with the community of believers, we see firsthand the vast difference of the obvious lacking network of support.

So it is with much gratitude to our Father I give thanks for His Grace, ever all-sufficient, and for His children who play a part in His merciful goodness.

We meet with the new radiation oncologist tomorrow at 8:30 AM.

As thy days, so shall your strength be. ~ Deuteronomy 33:25 KJV

Friday, December 15, 2006

We felt real comfortable with the new cancer center we went to yesterday and like our new radiation oncologist. He explained to us that chemotherapy works better for soft tissue cells and radiation works better for the bone, which is why we are adding this to our current chemo regimen. They don't normally like to administer both chemo and radiation simultaneously but in our case they don't wish to delay, either, so Vernon will receive daily radiation for two weeks in-between his current three-week chemo cycle. The radiation should decrease the pain and, of course, hopefully limit the cancers spread and growth. Breaking a bone is always a concern with weakened bones and due to the areas (hip and femur), loss of mobility is a concern. And once again we were given news of the disease in another area of his body; seems it is also in his other hip and leg so they want to radiate both of these areas. Perhaps this would explain the shooting pains Vernon has been having down both legs and in his back! Actually, they want to get a current bone scan to make sure they know all the areas to hit with the radiation. Scheduling is still in the process but it is expected we will begin radiation treatments the first week in the new year.

Sunday, December 17, 2006

Things that remind me that life is not as it used to be... some I resent, some I thank God for... I dislike that I have an Ensure magnet on my fridge... that I'm getting way too familiar with medical centers in multiple counties!... that my youngest often asks with trepidation, "Does Daddy have to go to the doctor today?"... that my children need to ask: "Who's taking care of us this time?" However, I am eternally grateful for a communion and peace with my Lord and companionship with my husband previously unequaled.

It's a very odd way to live, this reality that Vernon's life here on earth may not be long. It has begun to flow more in conversation, not yet as casually as one might discuss the weather, but God's grace extends beyond our comprehension.

Sometimes I think those of you whose lives intersect with ours might feel uncomfortable with our conversation. Feeling inadequate in how to express this but I thank you for sometimes allowing us to talk about death, for sometimes allowing us to not talk about it all.

The generosity of God's people leaves me astounded. Especially at this Christmas season, those remembering our children cause me to weep with both joy and sadness for both the reason and the season.

It seems I almost need watch what I find myself longing for, lest God grant it. I cannot tell you the times He has blessed in abundance above an actual "need." I found myself thinking this week how nice it would be if someone would bring some groceries once again. Got a call from some soul I've never even met the next day who then filled our table from Shady Maple.

And then there was the day last week that God prompted three different people to each give us a loaf of bread and it was three different kinds of bread - how neat is that!

A young mother we know of lies on her deathbed even now. She, too, has battled the beast of colon cancer, her battle ebbing and flowing the past few short years. It is hard to describe how this makes Vernon and I feel, knowing that, barring God's hand of mercy by physical healing, our time cometh.

Tuesday, December 19, 2006

It feels odd to be the one being Christmas "caroled" to. But we have been much encouraged by numerous groups of cheer spreading folks at our door and in our living room. Some brought cookies, some brought prayers, others poinsettias or roses, and some even brought a Christmas tree. We are so blessed this holiday season we often just sit and weep; we don't understand why God would be so good to us.

It seems a custom has sprung up around here of surprising folks in the "12 Days of Christmas" fashion. Each evening, early or late, there is a knock on our door with an anonymous gift representative of the rhyme. Our children are having so much fun with this. You should see them scramble when they hear the knock on the door. It is always fun to see what is left on our doorstep and then we look forward to the next night's offering. Much gratitude goes to whomever you are for bringing our children this joy in the midst of this sad time.

And here in dust and dirt, O here
The lilies of His love appear.

~ George Herbert

Friday, December 22, 2006

My cousin Rose from Chicago came to spend Christmas with us. She is such a blessing to have here and certainly helps to make this Christmas special for the children. She decorates and bakes with them and they revel in it.

Some friends gave us a gift certificate to Longwood Gardens. We enjoyed a lovely evening together there last night complete with dining in the Terrace Restaurant. The lights and flowers were stunning. Vernon enjoyed the use of the complementary motorized scooter.

And Vernon has graduated from one crutch to a cane now that he was given one the appropriate height and strength.

The past week, Vernon's pain has increased significantly enough to warrant higher doses of his pain medicine. In conversation with the doctor, he mentioned that, indeed, the last scan done months ago had showed spots on the pelvis and that is becoming a concern with the recently increased pain. He gave us some alarm symptoms to watch for and reiterated that radiation should be helpful to manage it. Chemo was cancelled for next week as they are concerned about the cell counts being down for radiation. We went for a nuclear bone scan today. We are almost afraid to know the results which we won't until we go in next week for the radiation "mapping".

To fear and not be afraid - that is the paradox of faith. ~ A.W. Tozer

Sunday, December 24, 2006

> Though for many Christmas speaks of joy and happiness.
> I know too well there are hurting hearts out there today
> who would rather the season just go away.
> Those who cannot see the tinsel and the mistletoe
> Through the haze of tears in their eyes.
> And though they sing:
> 'Glory to the newborn King'
> The heartaches of life here on earth
> can't help but sting.
> Oh, might they know the Sender of the babe
> cradles them this day.

Wednesday, December 27, 2006

Because it seems that so many times for us a doctor visit or phone call only brings more bad news of the cancer's whereabouts, it is not without apprehension that we go in this morning for radiation mapping with the recent bone scan in hand.

God constantly encourages us to trust Him in the dark.
'I will go before thee, and make the crooked places straight...'

~ A.W. Tozer

Wednesday, December 27, 2006

Plans are to begin a daily three-week radiation regimen next Thursday. Targeted areas: ribs, spine, hips, femur.

The doctor apologized today for the delay in treatments. He explained that since they are treating five different locations on Vernon's body, it is like treating five patients and they are going to work on the schedule again, but... In the meantime, he is going to put him on steroids for the bone pain and then Nexium for his stomach. He is concerned about his "wasting away" (yes, those were the exact awful words the doctor used). The doctor said there is no limit to the pain meds; that he just should just take what he needs.

Weep on if you are heavy, but do not weep without hope!
Weep on if you are afflicted, but do not think your affliction is in vain!
Weep on if you are mourning, but do not think that God ignores your tears!
Yes, weep if you must poor pilgrim, there is no shame in tears!

For now, if we must weep, let us not forget that tears are temporal;
let us not regret the privilege of life.
We will find strength to fly beyond these fountains of sorrow
so long as we view life through unflinching eyes gazed at eternity.

~ "A Trail of Tears" by B. K. Campbell

Saturday, December 30, 2006

Life has been a flurry of activity of late. Much to the children's chagrin, outside flurries not included.

My cousin Rose flew back to Chicago today. It is a grave understatement to say we will miss her. My brother and his family from New York pleasantly surprised us with their presence this weekend.

Vernon's pain has increased significantly. Two new meds added to the balancing act. It's not so simple as to just keep taking more pain meds as one needs, but to also live with the side effects.

You will never find Jesus so precious as when the world is
one vast howling wilderness. Then he is like a rose blooming
in the midst of the desolation, a rock rising above the storm.

~ Robert Murray M'Cheyne, 1813-1843

Monday, January 1, 2007

Thirteen years ago today, we stood before God and those witnesses we call our friends and family and vowed "for better or for worse, in sickness or in health" - never imagining what that would come to mean. I fight tears of sadness and resentment. I want so many more years together.

Vernon's bone pain continues to increase and we are challenged with managing it.

"We have tasted that the Lord is good" (Psalm 34:8), but we don't yet know how good He is. We only know that His sweetness makes us long for more." ~ C. H. Spurgeon

Tuesday, January 2, 2007

We seem to have the pain managed with taking mega doses of what's needed.

Though Vernon continues to be optimistic (he tells me he thinks we will yet celebrate our 25th together), I struggle with the memory of my mother's horrific suffering at the end and I dread what our future could hold. As I enter this new year, I must pray for joy to replace my fear.

We can walk up to any tomorrow knowing that God is there ahead of us waiting to anoint it with the oil of His grace. ~ Carolyn Lunn

Wednesday, January 3, 2007

Plans are to begin radiation tomorrow in Exton. We chose a closer radiation oncologist than where we are going for chemo in Philadelphia so that the daily trip will be more bearable. We were told that tomorrow they will do a "dry run" first, to ensure the markings are correctly placed (we've been having to touch up the x's on his body with a paint pen). Then they will tattoo with something more permanent once they ensure the treatment field is correct, and then he will receive his first radiation treatment to the five areas: rib, spine, both hips, and femur. The doctor told us that he should feel pain relief within a week so we are greatly anticipating that.

We remind ourselves of God's incredible mercy, new every morning, sufficient for each day.

Thursday, January 4, 2007

Radiation has begun and we are so grateful for the wisdom God has granted those in the medical world. Unfortunately, our daily time slot of 4:30 PM isn't ideal because of the children being out of school then. But we need to take the time they have available in the schedule and, because Vernon has multiple spots to radiate, he takes more than one slot so they've put us on the end of the day for the first week anyway. The second week we are scheduled for a more convenient time of 10:30 AM. The main side effect Vernon is to expect is tiredness, which will be nothing new.

> *Love's as hard as nails*
> *Love is nails:*
> *Blunt, thick, hammered through*
> *The medial nerves of One*
> *Who, having made us, knew*
> *The thing He had done,*
> *Seeing (with all that is)*
> *Our cross and his.*
>
> ~ C.S. Lewis

Sunday, January 7, 2007

We took the children along to radiation treatment Friday afternoon. Can't hurt to let the doctor see what we are fighting for! The children enjoyed the treats in the waiting room and the entire staff was endeared to them, as expected.

To give you a glimpse into our children's hearts, I share with you the following excerpts of our conversations in daily life…

A few nights ago when Vernon asked the children to say something describing God, Tov said: "He has a lot of grace." (Indeed, that is the substance of our existence these days!) And when Vernon told the children earlier this week that he will start radiation soon and that should help him feel better, Tia responded with: "Does that mean I won't have to cry anymore?" Kez got up one morning this week and said that she was crying in the night because she thought Daddy would die. But moments later she exclaimed "Daddy, they're singing my song!" "Great Is Thy Faithfulness" was playing on a CD (oh, may she always find her Heavenly Father to be so). Our eldest son does not often share the secrets of his soul but we know his heart to be tender and tried.

Our childrens' quality education being of utmost value to Vernon, we are helplessly humbled and genuinely grateful for the yet again anonymous donor who has paid the remainder of this year's tuition for our children at Veritas Academy!

Monday, January 8, 2007

Vernon's weight at the doctors today revealed he has actually lost a tad more weight so back to Ensure it is! "May Jesus Christ Be Praised", however, that we are seeing an improvement in his pain level; we take this to mean radiation is being effective! So far, no negative side effects of the radiation, either, though his midriff is an interesting tattooed array of symbols and letters.

Be joyful in hope, patient in affliction, faithful in prayer.
~ Romans 12:12 NIV

Wednesday, January 10, 2007

A sunny day... my husband behind the wheel and even pumping the gas for me... what could be better! Yes, if you're in Lancaster or Chester County these days, beware: Vernon is driving again. Doctors are understandably hesitant to give the okay with the amount of pain meds in his system but he pretty much said yesterday it would be ok (after asking Vernon if he knew about what time of the day it was to check his "sane-ability").

Vernon also started to walk some without his cane today! Praise God for these small but huge steps of encouragement!

Due to the amount of bone marrow they are radiating, low cell counts and risk of infection are high. Pray with us for Vernon's resistance to germs that could lead to trouble.

Jesus Christ can so interfere in a human life that it can look up and say, 'Bless the Lord, O my soul, and forget not all His benefits' even in the midst of sorrow or suffering. ~ Bob Pierce

Friday, January 12, 2007

> A dreary bitter cold day
> News of a friend moved to hospice to reach the end
> Tears hard to manage
> Words of hymns to nourish my soul
> Pink roses from a friend
> God is my hope and stay

These Clouds We So Much Dread

Saturday, January 13, 2007

The words of the hymn "Tell It To Jesus" minister to my soul in a way I'd never before imagined. I can identify as if they were written just for me… "Are you weary, are you heavy hearted?… Are you grieving over joys departed?… Do the tears flow down your cheeks unbidden?… Do you fear the gath'ring clouds of sorrow?… Are you anxious what shall be tomorrow?… Are you troubled at the thought of dying?"

Vernon is doing well right now, and we are enjoying our time together as never before. We are so grateful for the opportunity we have to nurture our relationships: with each other, with our children, with our Saviour and God. Living life with the reality of a terminal illness certainly brings a whole new meaning and depth. Not that we don't believe in miracles and in the power of God to bring us that blessing beyond belief. But whether or not He chooses to restore my husband's health, I will forever cherish what He has done and will continue to do in our lives right now. Yet it is a daily clinging, a daily bringing of my fears for the future to lay at His feet.

And I am blessed beyond belief with a Heavenly Father and Friend and earthly friends who care and express it daily. Thank you to all those whose tokens of concern mean more than you will ever know.

Cast thy burden on the Lord,
Only lean upon His word;
Thou wilt soon have cause to bless
His eternal faithfulness.

~ Anonymous Hymn

These Clouds We So Much Dread

Monday, January 15, 2007

    Saturday a bunch of guys came to work on Vernon's shop that he so desires to have finished so he can at least putter around home. Did that ever make his day, and the next, and the next! We are so impressed with the selfless giving of others time.

    This morning Kezia said to me, "Why don't you get rid of Daddy's cane? He doesn't need it anymore." Indeed, he is taking more and more steps without it (in the house anyway).

    Today's doctor's scale revealed another drop in weight. Made Vernon mad; he declares he is going to eat more frequently - and volume - to win this war on weight loss. He his now nearly sixty pounds less than he used to weigh. It's embarrassing to me that I now weigh as much as him; obviously I don't struggle with needing to gain.

    We are encouraged with the radiation effects as we have been able to reduce his pain meds by half from a week ago. We have morning radiation appointments this week, which makes it nicer for family life.

It's usually through our hard times, the unexpected and not-according-to-plan times, that we experience God in more intimate ways. We discover an unquenchable longing to know Him more. It's a passion that isn't concerned that life fall within certain predictable lines, but a passion that pursues God and knows He is relentless in His pursuit of each one of us.

    ~ Unknown Author

Tuesday, January 16, 2007

I will help thee, saith the Lord. ~ Isaiah 41:14 KJV

These Clouds We So Much Dread

This morning let us hear the Lord Jesus speak to each one of us: "I will help thee". It is but a small thing for Me, thy God, to help thee. Consider what I have done already. What! Not help thee? Why, I bought thee with My blood. What! Not help thee? I have died for thee, and if I have done the greater, will I not do the less? Help thee! It is the least thing I will ever do for thee; I have done more, and will do more. Before the world began I chose thee. I made the covenant for thee. I laid aside My glory and became a man for thee; I gave My life for thee; and if I did all this, I will surely help thee now. In helping thee, I am giving thee what I have bought for thee already. If thou hadst need of a thousand times as much help, I would give it thee; thou requires little compare with what I am ready to give. 'Tis much for thee to need, but it is nothing for me to bestow. "Help thee?" Fear not! If there were an ant at the door of thy granary asking for help, it would not ruin thee to give him a handful of thy wheat; and thou are nothing but a tiny insect at the door of My all sufficiency. "I will help thee."

O my soul, is not this enough? Dost thou need more strength than the omnipotence of the United Trinity? Does thou want more wisdom than exists in the Father, more love than displays itself in the Son, or more power than is manifest in the influence of the Spirit? Bring hither thine empty pitcher! Surely this well will fill it. Haste, gather up thy wants, and bring them there - thine emptiness, thy woes, they needs. Behold, this river of God is full for thy supply; what canst thou desire beside? Go forth, my soul, in this thy might. The Eternal God is thine helper!

~ C.H. Spurgeon

Tuesday, January 16, 2007

Our children are overnight with cousins tonight as we need to leave for Philly at 6 AM tomorrow for a CAT scan, then back to Exton for radiation.

Thursday, January 18, 2007

Today was our last day of radiation. The weeks have gone by quickly. Lord willing, if blood work remains positive, we will resume chemo next week as well as find out the results of the CAT scan.

The true spirit of prayer does not consist in asking for blessings, but in receiving Him who is the giver of all blessings, and in living a life of fellowship with Him. ~ Sundar Singh, 1889 - 1929

Friday, January 19, 2007

There are times I don't write because of time limitations, there are times I don't write because baring what is truly going on in our hearts and lives is too painful, there are times I don't write because I don't feel I have anything worthy to say. Most always I struggle with what to write and what not to write. But grateful I am for the prayers and communication this site solicits, and grateful I am for any glory that can go to our Heavenly Father who alone sustains us one day at a time.

One day at a time, with its failures and fears,
with its hurts and mistakes,
with its weakness and tears,
with its portion of pain and its burden of care.

One day at a time - but the day is so long,
and the heart is not brave and the soul is not strong;
O Thou merciful Christ, be thou near all the way;
give courage and patience and strength for the day.

One day at a time, and the day is His day;
He hath numbered its hours, though they haste or delay.
His grace is sufficient; we walk not alone;
as the day, so the strength that He giveth His own.

~ Annie J. Flint

Perhaps our children are getting used to their Mom and Dad weeping as easily as laughing, discussing cancer and future life possibilities as fluidly as outside temps or what's for dinner. At least they seem to be disappearing less and less when these potentially uncomfortable conversations occur.

One evening at supper this week, we had some therapeutic laughs around the table discussing Daddy's new temperament; guess you could call it our own caregiver support program.

And with what joy it fills our hearts to hear our four year old belting out the words to "Tell It To Jesus Alone" or her favorite requested song: "Great Is Thy Faithfulness."

Tia heard us discussing weight loss this week and wondered what that was. She says she doesn't remember Daddy when he wasn't like he is now. Oh my, sometimes children's brief memories can be a blessing and other times a true cause for sadness.

I marvel constantly at the goodness of God's people. Blessings beyond belief, time after time and right on time! This week, again, I was reminded of how God brought what I "needed" (such a relative word) nearly as soon as I thought how nice it would be or surprised me with something I wouldn't have even thought of. It is through tears and shame I struggle to understand why God would be so good to me. Perhaps my theology needs some honing.

Today the children had off school and Vernon wanted to take his boys skiing. Actually they opted for snowboarding and Vernon observed from a nice stuffed armchair in front of large glass windows that overlooked the slopes. Exceedingly grateful we are to the friends who accompanied us and patiently helped our beginners.

It is not without apprehension we wait for the CAT scan results next week. The doctor has told us that, due to the disruption of the chemo schedule (for bone surgery and then the radiation treatments), the CAT scan will not accurately portray the effectiveness of the latest chemo drug they are trying. Rather, it is to simply give them a current picture of how especially his liver is faring. Perhaps the news will be positive but it would be a first. Another new cause of concern is blood in his stool, along with some other alarming symptoms.

Faith takes these lives of ours out of our weak and fearful control and puts them in the hand of the Omnipotent. ~ Daniel Russell

Tuesday, January 23, 2007

We saw Vernon's bone surgeon for a follow-up visit. Basically, he just told us the x-ray showed the rod in his femur was straight (as if we're going to do something about it if it wasn't!) and that he could now jump out of a window if he wanted to and it wouldn't break (not that he was recommending that).

Tomorrow we return to Fox Chase for blood work, doctor visit and chemo. Talked with the doctor today a bit and of course they will do a thorough exam and review of both last week's CAT scan and of Vernon then, but he did mention that the scan showed cancer now in the lungs. Though we've come to dread these new bits of bad news, they no longer shock or consume us.

And when we spoke with the radiation oncologist this afternoon, he was nearly in tears. While it does make you feel good to know your doctors really care, it's also scary because you know they know more than you do. He confirmed the extensive cancer in Vernon's body and his exact words were that he "just hopes it doesn't claim his life sooner rather than later." He said the bleeding is most likely not from the radiation but from a tumor in the colon. Vernon has also been experiencing some extreme fatigue which, they tell us, is compliments of the radiation's toll on the body. In addition, he has been having increased discomfort in his abdomen and some other symptoms that the doctor will be addressing tomorrow. We do pray for the doctor's wisdom.

The doctor recommended we have our children talk to a social worker.

Should Thy mercy send me sorrow, toil and woe,
Or should pain attend me on my path below,
Grant that I may never fail Thy hand to see;
Grant that I may ever cast my care on Thee.

~ James Montgomery, 1834

Wednesday, January 24, 2007

Well, today's doctor visit wasn't too dismal. It wasn't exactly comforting either. The scales showed another weight loss; the CAT scan shows lesions in lungs not previously detected but suspected they were there. Some of the cancer in the liver had decreased while other areas had increased (hey, it's cancer - why should it make sense!). Liver not working as well as in past. Possibilities of some more bone metastases but need scan to

These Clouds We So Much Dread

confirm. There is a spot on the outside of the abdomen presumed to be the cancer coming to surface. However, the chemo should put a damper on the growth to all these areas.

They are continuing with the chemo drug he was previously on before we needed to delay treatments for bone surgery and then radiation. They cannot tell, due to the disruption in schedule, whether that drug is effective but are continuing with that one for a more consistent cycle to confirm effectiveness. They talked of adding another drug to the infusion today that is fairly new but its side effects were daunting enough (rash with itching, etc.) to cause us to hold off on that one until we see whether the current one is working. We expect to see some positive benefits in the near future. As usual it was a long ten-hour day away from home. We were grateful for Fagel's company and chauffeur services.

If I want only pure water, what does it matter to me whether it be brought in a vase of gold or of glass? What is it to me whether the will of God be presented to me in tribulation or consolation, since I desire and seek only the Divine will? ~ Francois de Sales, 1567 - 1622

Thursday, January 25, 2007

Last night, as tears streamed down our children's faces after yet another reality conversation had taken place concerning Daddy's cancer condition and God calling him to heaven, we recited a portion from Habakkuk we had learned as a family years ago, certainly never realizing then how close to home it would hit.

Though the fig tree does not bud
And there are no grapes on the vines,
Though the olive crop fails

And the fields produce no food,
Though there are no sheep in the pen
And no cattle in the stalls,
Yet I will rejoice in the Lord
I will be joyful in God my Saviour.
The Sovereign Lord is my strength;
He makes my feet like the feet of a deer,
He enables me to go on the heights.

~ Habakkuk 3:17-19 NIV

How we pray our children might grasp the goodness of their Sovereign Heavenly Father.

Saturday, January 27, 2007

Saturdays have begun to be a beehive of activity around here as more than a few good men descend upon this place and work to get Vernon's shop completed for him. I looked out over our drive today at the half dozen work trucks, trailers and skid loader with a lump in my throat and tears in my eyes. I am simply overwhelmed with the sacrificial kindness these men extend toward my husband. While it is disappointing for him not to be out there doing it himself, he helps with what he can and the rest of the time observes the progression with immense and increasing satisfaction from the living room window overlooking the construction scene.

Sometimes I hear Vernon praising God after he reads a normal temp on his thermometer. Chemo patients are required to keep a close eye on their temp. Anything over 100.5 warrants an ER visit. We surely do take much less for granted than ever before. Vernon continues to be very, very weary; a supposed combination of radiation after effects, current chemo and pain med side effects.

Think not that even with brevity of life looming that marital friction does not occur; however, apologies and forgiveness come quicker. There is simply no time to hold grudges.

I've been thinking a lot lately how it would be if we could see life as Jesus did with His perspective of eternity when He lived on this earth - the true knowledge of knowing that life here below with its sorrows and pain is brief and insignificant in light of eternity with the Father.

If I say to you that no one has time to finish, that the longest human life leaves a man, in any branch of learning, a beginner, I shall seem to you to be saying something quite academic and theoretical. You would be surprised if you knew how soon one begins to feel the shortness of the tether: of how many things, even in middle life, we have to say, 'No time for that,' 'Too late now' and 'Not for me.' But Nature herself forbids you [young people] to share that experience. A more Christian attitude, which can be attained at any age, is that of leaving futurity in God's hands. We may as well, for God will certainly retain it whether we leave it to Him or not. ~ C. S. Lewis

Monday, January 29, 2007

Vernon has taken a turn for the worse - liver issues. We are headed out the door to Brandywine Hospital.

As fear threatens to consume me, the prayer I breathe is: "God, into your hands, I commit my husband."

The swift changes of life amaze us. The brevity of life startles and appalls us. ~ Daniel Russell

Monday, January 29, 2007

Due to Vernon's liver not functioning well, the ammonia level in his blood is elevated which causes him to be sleepy and disoriented. They are keeping him in the hospital tonight and hopefully he can go home tomorrow with some home nursing help. The children are overnight at their cousins.

Tuesday, January 30, 2007

We are just home from the hospital and needless to say rejoicing as there is no place like home (especially not a hospital!). Vernon is doing okay. I will update in more detail later as able. Through exhausted tears of appreciation I express my gratitude for the multitude of prayers and expressions of concern the past twenty-four hours!

Tuesday, January 30, 2007

This entry promises to be a bit long and cumbersome but for those who want medical details, this is for you…

We left home around 11:00 yesterday morning for the hospital. Vernon had been becoming increasingly unable to stay awake as well as disoriented. We spent until 6 PM in the ER where they did a CAT scan to the head to confirm no cancer activity in brain, an ultrasound on the liver to check the size of tumors there. Blockage of bile ducts was a possibility. The test showed no blockage. However the blood work did confirm suspicions of both reduced liver function and consequential elevated amounts of ammonia. We also found out that, actually, last week at Fox Chase when they gave him chemo, they had only given one-half the dose due to liver function and size of the growth (once again we are incredulous at how the medical world can withhold truth from you till in their timing).

After reaching our room, we were turned over to our family doctor who had the privilege of giving us the "low-down". He wanted to know from us how much more we were willing to do to extend Vernon's life, and at what cost. His opinion is that, were we to do nothing at all, Vernon could reach a comatose state in a matter of days and it wouldn't be too many days following that for death to occur due to liver failure. The other option was to increase a medicine to induce diarrhea to help keep the ammonia levels down. Unfortunately, there is no guarantee that this will be effective and then, of course, there is the undesirable side effects of loose stools. Also, it seems questionable whether his liver can actually utilize the chemo if he is able to receive more. Were we to "fight it", the doctor suspects he might live a few more months at best, but the quality of that extended time is questionable.

Whichever route we were going to choose, going home was non-optional; Vernon *hates* the hospital and couldn't figure out how he had gotten in there. Whether we went home with hospice to keep him comfortable, or home with visiting nurses to keep IV and meds going to keep fighting, it could be done at home.

Immense gratitude to those who left phone messages on my cell phone in the hospital and for those late-night visitors (can you believe they let our pastor and elder in the hospital at midnight?). It was most annoying to not have internet access while there and a friend posted the brief post for me last night.

Throughout the past days God's mercy drops were evident. We had a friend who worked at the hospital so between her help and Vernon being in his condition, we received utmost compassion and extraordinary kindness our entire hospital stay. I was even allowed to sleep in the empty bed in his room. Well, "sleep" maybe isn't the correct word. It was a long, difficult night; Vernon up a lot with his trips to the bathroom that he needed help with.

Well, the conversation with the doctor on his round this morning was not nearly as acutely discouraging. He is saying now that they still need to rule out pain med build-up and sodium level as reason for sleepiness. It seems now there could be three reasons for his present condition: 1) liver failure, 2) sodium levels, 3) pain med and sleeping pill build up (due to his liver not assimilating the meds as it should have).

Well, the blood work finally came back. It showed ammonia levels had dropped from 102 to 75 (normal being 45). It showed Sodium back up to normal level due to IV fluids they gave him. So now they need to rule out pain med and sleeping pill build-up. They are cutting out and back on much of his meds, including water pills for his ascites (fluid in abdomen), in hopes to keep sodium steady and him from dehydration.

At first they had told us he would need an IV at home but, thankfully, that is no longer necessary if we can keep him drinking. Now it is going to be a waiting game for the next day or so as we wait for excess meds to be rid from his system, and they can then tell whether his present condition is indeed from that or completely from liver failure.

And just what is Vernon's present condition? It is hard for him to stay awake, he says off the wall stuff and sometimes has difficulty remembering what day it is, etc. Then, other times, he isn't too far from normal, other than being tired and wobbly. It should go without saying this is very scary for me to see my husband this way, not to mention confusing to the children. We continue to covet your prayers as we see what the next days unfold and as we weigh decisions before us now.

Wednesday, January 31, 2007

Praise God from whom all blessings flow! Vernon seems better this morning! He hasn't said anything weird yet. We are much encouraged!

Talking to the doctor this morning, he is wanting to wait a few days of observation yet to make some diagnosis decisions.

Wednesday, January 31, 2007

For you faithful prayer warriors - and how grateful I am for each one!

Vernon seems to be becoming increasingly weaker and more tired. He is no longer disoriented, though, so that is a blessing. We are still very much in a balancing act with his meds. Presently he is experiencing considerable discomfort from ascites (fluid in abdomen).

Vain is the chiming of forgotten bells
That the wind sways above a ruined shrine.
Vainer his voice in whom no longer dwells
Hunger that craves immortal Bread and Wine.

Light songs we breathe, that perish with our breath,
Out of our lips that have not kissed the rod.
They shall not live who have not tasted death.
They only sing who are struck dumb by God.

~ Joyce Kilmer, 1886 - 1918

Wednesday, January 31, 2007

This afternoon's house call from our family doctor resulted in the addition of a new med as, with impaired liver function, bacteria in intestines can be troublesome. We pray for a good night's rest for Vernon tonight.

I came down today with a bad head cold and sore throat and thus am not at all oozing with compassion and patience for the needs of my family. And we really cannot afford for Vernon to catch this. However frustrated I am at the timing of me getting sick, I must remind myself constantly of God's complete sovereignty in all things. Thank you for your prayers in even this matter.

One of Vernon's sisters spent the night last night and another one is coming tonight so that I can get a good night's rest. What a blessing!

I must tell Jesus all of my trials; I cannot bear these burdens alone…
~ Elisha Hoffman

Thursday, February 1, 2007

Vernon feels much better this morning, the discomfort and pressure in his abdomen is less and he doesn't seem quite as weak and weary.

The effectual fervent prayer of a righteous man availeth much.
~ James 5:16 KJV

Thursday, February 1, 2007

It is incredible what a difference twenty-four hours can make! Yesterday at this time, my husband was miserable and looked near death. But today he was even outside briefly "dombling around " (his words) and he seems to be continually improving. It is puzzling, medically speaking, but we thank God for the reprieve. And I feel very much better - thanks all you dear folks who prayed for me and one even brought me chicken soup! It truly was a nourishment, both for body and soul.

Our day has been chock-full of visitors and helpers; we've benefited from the services of a massage therapist, a house cleaner, suppers and grocery bearers, and other visitors offering support and encouragement.

My Dad and his wife surprised us from Florida today. And three of Vernon's-out-of state sisters are coming for the weekend.

For the joy of human love,
Brother, sister, parent, child,
Friends on earth, and friends above;
For all gentle thoughts and mild:
Lord of all, to thee we raise
This our hymn of grateful praise.

~ Folliott S. Pierpoint

Friday, February 2, 2007

Pardon me for not writing an update this morning... sometimes it just hurts too much.

Another frank discussion with the doctor today... faith... hope... denial... reality - seem a blur. How does one live with a life expectancy of your loved one mere weeks?

But I know whom I have believed and am persuaded that He is able to keep that which I've committed unto Him against that day.

~ Daniel W. Whittle, 1840-1901

Saturday, February 3, 2007

Vernon is doing so well, it makes it difficult to believe the accuracy of the doctor's prognosis. He was up and going all day - even went to the hardware store and away for supper! But do continue to pray for him to sleep well at night.

Had a precious time of sharing with his seven sisters and parents gathered here this morning.

We are gaining much peace in our souls by singing the good ole hymns lately. We ask many of our visitors to help sing.

Thou knowest, Lord, the weariness and sorrow
Of the sad heart that comes to Thee for rest;
Cares of to-day, and burdens for tomorrow,
Blessings implored, and sins to be confessed:
I come before Thee at Thy gracious word,
And lay them at Thy feet,- Thou knowest, Lord.

~ Jane Borthwick, 1813-1897

Monday, February 5, 2007

Vernon is having a good morning. Yesterday started out a bit hard but then we were able to go to church in the morning, which was an answer to prayers. Further discussion with the doctor - another prescription resumed - life is expected to continue as is with ups and downs as we regulate his medications for his optimum comfort level. He is having swelling in his legs and feet now which is of some concern.

Father knows best!

*Our fathers disciplined us for a little while as they
thought best; but God disciplines us for our good,
that we may share in His holiness." (Hebrews 12:10)
"What God, our Father wills, is best.
When He wills sickness, sickness in better than health.
When He wills weakness, weakness is better than strength.
When He wills want, want is better than wealth.
When He wills reproach, reproach is better than honor.
When He wills death, death is better than life.
As God is wisdom itself, and so knows that which is
best; so He is goodness itself, and therefore cannot
do anything but that which is best--therefore remain
silent before the Lord.*

~ *The Mute Christian Under the Smarting Rod*, Thomas Brooks, 1659

Tuesday, February 6, 2007

Another conversation with our doctor this morning as we continue to puzzle over Vernon's condition. Our family doctor and our oncologist at Fox Chase consulted together and are thinking now that it was quite probable the chemo Vernon had received prior to his hospitalization is what caused his decline. Something about the chemo and protein and liver function. They want to continue to monitor his progress on a day-by-day basis and then we will meet with our Fox Chase doctor next Wednesday to discuss matters and the wisdom of pursuing treatment. They are saying now that, if indeed it was the chemo that was the cause of his decline, we may increase his life expectancy to several months. Whew, what a relief!

Oh how great a peace and quietness would he possess who should cut off all vain anxiety and place all his confidence in God.
~ Thomas A. Kempis

Thursday, February 8, 2007

Vernon is doing well. He is adamant on getting his barn finished for his boys and spends much of his time working towards that end. It is an odd way to live - painting windows in between funeral and burial plan conversations. Healthwise, he is doing fairly well. He does have extreme swelling in his feet and ankles but doesn't allow it to hinder him from getting around too much. His eyes look less yellow than they had. He continues to take the meds to keep ammonia levels down and we anxiously await our oncologist appointment next week. Please do continue to pray for good night's rest for him.

"He will quiet you by His love" (Zephaniah 3:17 ESV) is certainly our experience in these uncertain and potentially frightening times. By God's mercy alone, we are able to experience a peace and submission to His plan that can only be attributed to His grace. Not that there is not many a time I don't plead for Him to keep me from allowing my thoughts to drift to days ahead and how I will ever manage to cope. But as for a franticness of what should be talked about or done in what could be our last days together, we are able to experience a spirit of sereneness and can honestly await our celestial summons in peace. I am oh so grateful God has given me a security in both my marriage and my salvation that is of eternal comfort.

And my soul complaineth not,
For no pain or fears dismay her;
Still she clings to God in faith,

Trusts Him though He seem to slay her.
Tis when flesh and blood repine,
Sun of joy, Thou canst not shine.

~ Johann J. Winckler, 1670-1722

Sunday, February 11, 2007

Naturally, talk of heaven finds its way into many of our discussions. Kezia said recently, "I wish I could get sick like Daddy and go to heaven, too." And I tell Vernon it is not fair he gets to go before me and especially when I am frustrated with the children and distressed at the thought of raising them alone. Another time, when Tia was in tears over the idea of Daddy dying and I assured her we would all be together there someday, through sobs she inquired: "When?!" I said God would make it seem not long and she wailed again, "How do you know?!" My passionate prayer is that my children will turn to their God for comfort and not away from Him in confusion or bitterness. Yet I gratefully acknowledge God's grace is sufficient for even this.

I have such respect and admiration for our family doctor who so graciously accepts my nearly-daily calls on his cell phone. Though I don't always get the answers to my questions I would like to hear, I appreciate his honesty even when he simply says: "I do not know." We continue to need to regulate Vernon's meds daily for ammonia level control. Though the swelling in his feet and legs is significant, increasing his fluid pills could cause dehydration so, for now, he must live with the discomfort and inconvenience this causes. The past few days he is again struggling with extreme sleepiness and we are hopeful it is a mere buildup of pain meds again and are working on regulating them.

It could be the ammonia levels as well as liver failure progresses but, as always... "One day at a time, sweet Jesus..."

Tuesday, February 13, 2007

Vernon seems to be weaker the past few days with a difficult-to-explain, general feeling of discomfort. Please pray I can be strong for the children and Vernon. It's harder on everyone when mom is weak.

How it nourishes my soul to hear of the faithful prayers of the saints and sometimes wonder where we'd be without them. I must also thank the many of you who write either in the guest book (which is such an encouragement to Vernon) and the personal e-mails to me. I apologize that lately I do not have the time to reply to each one as I used to. Please know that I value all correspondence even though I am unable to express that personally.

'What Thou wilt, when Thou wilt, how Thou wilt.' I had rather speak these three sentences from my heart in my mother tongue than be master of all the languages in Europe. ~ John Newton, 1725-1807

Tuesday, February 13, 2007

What a balance there seems to be between resting in what God has ordained and trying to do all that man can do. No doubt I exerted some unnecessary frustration this day over some doctor calls (three different doctors to be exact!) and a decision made to not make the trek to Fox Chase tomorrow. Weather here is a winter wonderland and the forecast for tomorrow is more of the same. My dear doctor-brother from Michigan reminded and admonished me gently that, realistically, whether we make our

Philadelphia appointment tomorrow or not does not bind God's hands in how He chooses to heal or not heal Vernon's body. And our oncologist confirmed by phone conversation as well today that the likelihood of Vernon's body tolerating or benefiting from more chemo at this point is unlikely enough to not merit the trip. We do plan to go get blood work done at our family doctor in the next day or so (roads permitting) and from that they will have a better idea of where his levels (ammonia, liver function, blood counts) are since the last blood work done was several weeks ago now.

I hear the Saviour say, 'Thy strength indeed is small,
Child of weakness watch and pray, Find in Me thine all in all.

~ Elvine M. Hall

Wednesday, February 14, 2007

Snow, sleet and ice abound here in our parts of the woods.
Pray against discouragement for Vernon.
Never being one eager for hugs and hearts, I've never held a fondness for Valentines Day but, in keeping with the day, I'll offer this...

Love does not consist in gazing at each other but in looking together in the same direction. ~ Antoine de Saint-Exupery

That "same direction" in our case is *Heaven* - our eternal home!

Thursday, February 15, 2007

Doctor this morning gave Vernon mere days to live. Hospice is coming out. More details later.

Not mindless of the growing years
Of care and loss and pain,
My eyes are wet with thankful tears
For blessings that remain.

~ J.G. Whittier, 1807-1892

Thursday, February 15, 2007

What "a day the Lord hath made." (Psalms 118:24 KJV)

I feel like I should explain how it came to today's news. As I mentioned earlier in the week, Vernon had been becoming increasingly more fatigued and a general, overall feeling of discomfort. Yesterday, though I was eager to get him to the doctor, roads did not permit. He spent much of yesterday on the couch and by last night he was beginning to feel dizzy and disoriented. This morning he was having difficulty catching his breath so we got the drive plowed out so we could go into our family doctor. After examining Vernon, he soberly told us he thought his days were few as liver failure had accelerated. He arranged for hospice to come in. The nurse was here this afternoon for several hours. Family will take turns staying here. We may need to bring in oxygen tomorrow but hope to maintain comfort with only meds. What is expected with the progression of lack of liver function is that he will become increasingly sleepier and eventually lapse into a coma. He is, at this point, tired and confused but still able to be up and around. The nurse actually thought he was doing too well to die that soon.

Vernon is now ready to go home to meet His Maker and Savior. I am ready for him to go. I can imagine the welcoming committee there will be grand.

We have known ever since Vernon's original diagnosis in July that his cancer was terminal. We were told then that, with his condition, he could live five years but that two years was the average. In the seven months following that, with continued findings of new metastasis, we realized that time had most likely shortened. Yet knowing and experiencing are two quite different things. Knowing your days are numbered (how we all live as if they are not!), but then watching and feeling one's life ebb is stark reality.

Thank you for respecting our family time during these days. E-mails and guest book entries are most appreciated.

There is no instrument whose broken and untuned strings he cannot make discourse sweet strains - even a heart collapsed with grief.
~ Octavius Winslow, 1808-1878

Friday, February 16, 2007

Vernon seems to be in a pre-coma condition. The hospice nurse tonight said she does not expect him to live past the weekend.

Lord, the one You love is sick.
~ John 11:3 NIV

Friday, February 16, 2007

Prayer at the bedside of a dying believer

Ever blessed God, we rejoice to know that our times are in Your hands. The Lord gives us our lives--the Lord has a sovereign right to take them away. Give us grace to say, 'Blessed be the name of the Lord!' Do look down in great mercy on Your servant, whom You are about to take to Yourself. Let him know, that, leaning on Jesus, the sting is plucked away from death, and the grave is robbed of its victory. Oh, ever-living Redeemer, great 'Abolisher of Death,' who has brought life and immortality to light by the Gospel--smooth his dying pillow—let Your voice be heard, saying, 'Fear not, it is I; be not afraid!' Grant relief from suffering. Give him a peaceful entrance into glory; may Your angels even now be waiting to waft him to Your presence. May he know that You are faithful who has promised, 'Lo, I am with you always, even unto the end of the world!'

Forgive, oh, forgive all his past sins. May this be the one glorious truth to which his soul clings in a dying hour, 'The blood of Jesus Christ, God's Son, cleanses from all sin.' Lord, may Your own blessed soul-sustaining peace be his. In a few more moments, he will wake up in heaven--sorrow and sighing shall have fled away forever. May he feel that to depart and to be with Christ is indeed far better. Hear us, good Lord, for Jesus' sake. Amen.

~ John MacDuff, 1885

Saturday, February 17, 2007

We are singing as a family gathered around Vernon as he nears life's end:

My latest sun is sinking fast,
My race is nearly run;
My strongest trials now are past,
My triumph is begun.
Refrain:

Oh, come, angel band,
Come and around me stand;
Oh, bear me away on your snowy wings
To my eternal home;
Oh, bear me away on your snowy wings
To my eternal home.
I know I'm near the holy ranks
Of friends and kindred dear—
I hear the waves on Jordan's banks,
The crossing must be near.
I've almost reached my heav'nly home,
My spirit loudly sings;
Thy holy ones, behold, they come!
I hear the noise of wings.
Oh, bear my longing heart to Him,
Who bled and died for me;
Whose blood now cleanses from all sin,
And gives me victory.

~ "Oh, Come Angel Band" by Jefferson Hascall, 1860

Saturday, February 17, 2007

The children and I, together with Vernon's parents and most of his siblings, witnessed Vernon's peaceful passage from earth to glory around 8:30 PM.

The desire of our eyes has been taken away by a stroke! The shadows of death have unexpectedly fallen around us! Oh forbid that we should rebel under the rod, and refuse to be comforted. Let us glorify You 'in the fires!' Let us feel that if we are Your children, there is not a drop of wrath, in that cup of sorrow; but all is love, infinite love! We would see no hand but Yours.

You gave us our blessings--and You have a supreme and inalienable right to take them away! 'Even so, Father, for it seems good in Your sight.'

O Lord God Almighty, though Your way may sometimes seem to be in the sea, and Your path in the deep waters, and Your judgments unsearchable--yet nothing can happen by accident or chance. All is the unerring dictate of Your infinite wisdom and unchanging faithfulness and love. 'This also comes from the Lord Almighty,' who is ever 'excellent in working.' Often we cannot discern, through our tears, the rectitude and love of Your afflictive dispensations. Often are we led to say, with trembling hearts, 'Truly, You are a God who hides Yourself.' But all is well. We could not wish our concerns in better hands, than in Yours.

You cannot send one trial that is unnecessary, or light one spark in the furnace that might be spared. We will be silent, we will not open our mouths, because You are the one who has done this! Man may err, and has often erred. But, O unerring God--the Judge of all the earth must do right! We would seek to lie submissive at Your feet, and say in unmurmuring resignation, 'May Your will be done.'

Our earnest prayer, blessed God, is, that this severe trial may be sanctified to us all. We have need of such a blow--to remind us that this earth is not our rest. We were leaning on the creature--we were disowning and undeifying the Great Creator. You would not leave us to ourselves, to settle on our lees. You saw the need of Fatherly chastisement, to bring back our alien and truant hearts to Yourself. Oh, may we listen to our Father's voice. May we feel it to be a loud voice, and yet full of gentle tenderness. May it rouse within each of us the question, 'What will You have me to do?' May we 'arise and call upon our God!' Thus may this very affliction, which, for the present, seems not to be joyous but grievous, nevertheless afterward yield the peaceable fruit of righteousness.

Let us hear Jesus' voice of encouragement and love, sounding amid the stillness of the death-chamber, and from the depths of the sepulcher, 'Don't be afraid! I am the First and the Last. I am the living one who died. Look, I am alive forever and ever! And I hold the keys of death and the grave!'

O Helper of the helpless, Comforter of all who are cast down, better and dearer than the dearest and best of earthly relatives--give us that grace which You have promised specially in seasons of weakness. May we realize the truth of Your own precious promise, 'As your day--so shall your strength be.'

May this thought reconcile us to bear all and suffer all--that we shall soon be done with this present evil world--and be with our God, and that forever and ever! Hide us meanwhile, in the clefts of the Smitten Rock, until this and all other of earth's calamities are over and past. May we trust Your heart-- where we cannot trace Your hand! We wait patiently for the great day of disclosures, when all shall be revealed; and all be found redounding to the praise and the glory of Your great name!

Hear us, blessed God. All that we ask, is for the sake of Your dear Son- -our only Lord and Savior. Amen.

"Prayer for a time of bereavement" from John MacDuff 'Family Prayers', 1885

Sunday, February 18, 2007

A dear friend wrote this morning: "To think that Vernon got his heart's desire to wake up Sabbath morning in the unveiled presence of His King…"

The decision has been made for the funeral to be held Tuesday afternoon.

Wednesday, February 21, 2007

As time permits, I shall share morsels of the mercies God granted in the last days of Vernon's life for, truly, "Mercy there was great and grace was free." Also plan to post about the funeral for those of you faithful pray-ers who were unable to attend.

For now I am clinging to the family that remains and trying to stifle a sense of panic for when the flowers fade and the house rings silent; when the ache becomes suffocating and the stab of pain can not be anesthetized by activity and denial.

The following was written by my cousin, Rose Miller and printed in the funeral program:

Vernon grew up in Honey Brook. He was the fourth of nine children. After high school he worked on the family farm for some years then developed an interest in horticulture and took several years of landscaping courses at Penn State. He then began his own business and his creative talent soon became a favorite of many. He married Sharon at age 31 and his children soon became his passion in life. The birth of his children caused Vernon to reevaluate his life, priorities and values, and he began to delve into scriptural study and discipleship with newly found vigor. His children seemed to open to Vernon a window to things of eternal value and he was often found reading, studying, teaching and singing about God's truth and amazing love. His songs were contagious and his children picked up the chorus, learning lessons of God and grace and life through their family worship times and spontaneous hymn singing throughout their daily routines together. Vernon greatly valued his children's education and loved to participate in their homework, school projects and after-school activities. In addition he was frequently seen collaborating with them in projects such as building a barn, creating an ice rink and teaching them to care for and enjoy the many plants and flowers he had embellished his home with. He loved the out of doors (but not the cold), and tackled a day of hard work with the same vigor with which he wrestled his boys on the living room floor after coming home. His creative talent and passion for perfection resulted in gardens bursting with floral profusion, and a family impressioned by his energy, fierce devotion and sheer love of life. And like the gardens he created he will remain alive in the hearts of his wife, children and loved ones, nurtured by sacred memories, and watered by God's gracious healing.

The following was written by Craig Mattson, husband of Vernon's sister, Rhoda.

"For Vernon's Wake, Towards His Waking"

"We believe... in the resurrection of the body"

Father have mercy, but we miss his hands,
blunt-edged fingers, relentless on the spade
and pruning shear, resting for slow moments
on stone and shoot, hearing eloquence some-
where deep in tree and soil.

Kind Christ look on us, lonely for his eyes,
the countenance he bent, by turns grimly
on scrimmage line, kindly on cheek of child,
the smile's crow feet spreading from edge of eye,
the brow lifted in laughter.

When house is still, Spirit, we ask your pity
for turning at some sound we take for him,
his murmuring, the readiness of it
so low, we ask him to say again what
hope he had given voice.

Be gentle with us and make good your word
that all of him we knew, or thought we knew,
muscled grasp, rolling stride, and rasp of voice,
that these, remade, shall be gathered into
your company, and ours.

Friday, February 23, 2007

More about the funeral…

Our former pastor, Steve Estes, put it together and led the service in a most beautiful manner. Our pastor, Steve Arrick, preached the message on Colossians Chapter One, which was the chapter Vernon was currently memorizing. There were scriptures of sorrow and scriptures of hope that were read. Songs that have become quite precious to our family these past months, which the children and I were adamant needed to be included in the funeral and graveside service, included both hymns of crying out to God and hymns of trust and praise: "I Need Thee Every Hour", "God, Be Merciful to Me", "Oh God Our Help", "God Moves in a Mysterious Way", "Lord, with Glowing Heart I'd Praise Thee", "Tell It to Jesus", "All the Way My Savior Leads Me", "Be Still My Soul", "Rock of Ages Cleft for Me", and "Great Is Thy Faithfulness".

Tia (age six) wrote a note for her Daddy to put in the casket. It read: "I love you Dad and I know you having a good time in heaven."

We did much singing the final weeks and days of Vernon's life. There was one song that was a favorite of his (he requested it be sung at his funeral). It was a song that he was best at starting and when he was at the point physically where he was no longer participating in our singing, I told him we needed him to start this song for us; he managed the first line. It was the last song he helped sing:

> *Lord, with glowing heart I'd praise Thee,*
> *For the bliss Thy love bestows,*
> *For the pardoning grace that saves me,*
> *And the peace that from it flows:*
> *Help, O God, my weak endeavor;*
> *This dull soul to rapture raise:*
> *Thou must light the flame, or never*
> *Can my love be warmed to praise.*
> *Praise, my soul, the God that sought thee,*
> *Wretched wanderer, far astray;*
> *Found thee lost, and kindly brought thee*
> *From the paths of death away;*
> *Praise, with love's devoutest feeling,*
> *Him Who saw thy guilt-born fear,*
> *And the light of hope revealing,*
> *Bade the blood-stained cross appear.*
> *Praise thy Savior God that drew thee*
> *To that cross, new life to give,*
> *Held a blood sealed pardon to thee,*
> *Bade thee look to Him and live.*
> *Praise the grace whose threats alarmed thee,*
> *Roused thee from thy fatal ease;*
> *Praise the grace whose promise warmed thee,*
> *Praise the grace that whispered peace.*
> *Lord, this bosom's ardent feeling*
> *Vainly would my lips express.*
> *Low before Thy footstool kneeling,*
> *Deign Thy suppliant's prayer to bless:*
> *Let Thy grace, my soul's chief treasure,*

Love's pure flame within me raise;
And, since words can never measure,
Let my life show forth Thy praise.

~ Francis Scott Key, 1819

Friday, February 23, 2007

There was a man, a recent friend of Vernon's, who devoted himself to come on a weekly basis during Vernon's illness to spend time with him, reading scripture and praying. Those visits always meant so much to my husband. The following prayer was written and read by that friend, Dave Stoltzfus, at the funeral...

O Lord, You have been our dwelling place throughout all generations. Before the mountains were born or You brought forth the earth and the world, from everlasting to everlasting You are God. You turn men back to dust, saying, 'Return to dust, O sons of men.' For a thousand years in Your sight are like a day that has just gone by, or like a watch in the night. You sweep men away in the sleep of death; they are like the new grass of the morning – though in the morning it springs up new, by evening it is dry and withered (Psalm 90:1-6).

Lord you have blessed us by creating this man and leaving him on this earth for 44 ½ years. We wish it were longer but You know – You are the Wise One. We thank You for how he reflected Your image on this earth. No – he was far from perfect but, boy, did we see Your work in his life. His love for Your Word, his love for his children, his love for his wife, his faithfulness, his honesty, his zeal for Your glory - these are all qualities that came from You. His love of work, his love of fun, his competitive spirit – these were from You. Thanks for making him the way You did.

But because of how You made him and how You worked in him, now that You've taken him, the hole left is big. Lord, we need You to fill it as only You can. Close friends of Vernon's feel a deep loss. Many have seen Your hand work even through his sickness and death like never before. This is Your goodness and how You turn Satan on his head. Thank you that this room is filled with people who are thinking about You and about eternity instead of work or sports or the weather. Thank you that thousands upon thousands of prayers have been offered to You over the past months because of Vernon's sickness, a sickness and death ordained by You. But even in the midst of the good there is a deep loss. Lord, only You can fill that void and we ask You to do just that for every relative and friend of this dear man. And if any do not know You, use his death to bring them to life.

Vernon's parents, Ben and Emma, are experiencing the most difficult of trials — the loss of a son. Lord, we thank You for them and the many qualities taught Vernon by them. Lord, when the burden is bigger than they think they can bear, help them to remember that You too lost a Son, and that Your Son's death made it possible for their son's death to be a bearable event. And may Your love to them be more real than ever before because of it.

And Lord, I pray for Linda and Ivan and Liz and Vernon (I don't have to pray for Vernon. He's doing quite well) and Kathy and Verda and Verna and Rhoda and Rosie. These dear people have lost a brother, a caring brother, a special brother. No more free advice on landscaping, no more free work on the patio. Family gatherings will never be the same. Lord, when this family gathers and sees the empty chair and feels the empty space; when they think of Vernon, may they think of You and be reminded of Your awesome deeds among them. May Your glory which Vernon cared so much for be more evident among them with Vernon gone then when he was here.

And Lord, our hearts ache for these children, four gifts from You. You promise to be a Father to the fatherless. Jedidiah, Tovi, Tia and Kezia are fatherless and this by Your hand; by Your sovereign will. We claim Your promise Lord, we know that Vernon, as good of a dad as he was, his fathering pales in comparison to Yours. Would You gather them up in Your arms and give them each exactly what they need. Jed who contains his feelings, Tovi who lets them out, Tia and Kezia, who have already experienced what many people don't until they're my age. May the loss of their dad make them more like their dad and more like their Heavenly Father. Lord, please provide for them through Your people, and what we cannot and where we fail, will You cover for us? We need You to do this because we are weak and we are sinners.

And lastly, Lord, for Sharon – You have taken from her the two dearest people she knows. Her mother some years ago and now her husband. Lord, this we don't understand. We know Your Word says that all things work together for good for those who love You and are called according to Your purpose. Because You say it, we believe it. But boy, it's hard. It's hard for us to see but it must be almost impossible for Sharon. How can it be good to lose a husband in the prime of his life? We trust You Lord and Sharon trusts You. But, it's not easy and we easily slip. Help Sharon, Lord, as she thinks of the future to trust You today and realize that tomorrow is in Your hands. Her breadwinner is gone. How will they eat? You are the Bread of life. I have never seen the righteous forsaken or their children begging for bread. How will she be able to provide education for the kids which was so very important to Vernon? You own the cattle on a thousand hills. Nothing is too hard for You. Lord, Sharon needs faith, grace, perseverance and the ability to trust You even when there is only fog ahead. And Lord, in the midst of all of this, I hope it's not overreach to ask You to give her joy. Lord, make her glad according to the days You have afflicted her. Please do this for her, Lord. You have enriched our lives greatly over the past months by her journal and unpretentious writings. Your grace has been displayed in a very rare and glorious manner. You have blessed us greatly through her. Now we ask You to bless her through us. And when we fail, do it without us.

Now unto Him who is able to keep you from stumbling, you – Ben and Emma, Linda, Ivan, Liz, Kathy, Verda, Verna, Rhoda and Rosie - Jed, Tovi, Tia and Kezia. Now unto Him who is able to keep you – Sharon from stumbling and to make you stand in the presence of His glory (with Vernon) blameless with great joy. To the only God our Savior, through Jesus Christ our Lord, be glory, majesty, dominion and authority, before all time and now and forever. Amen (Jude 1:24, 25).

Part Three
These Clouds

Saturday, February 24, 2007

"How are the children doing?" is a question often asked. To that my answer would be simply: I see God's grace in them, I think they are doing remarkably well, bearing in mind several things: one of which is that we have mourned the loss of our Daddy over many months. The Daddy who left us last week was not the same Daddy we knew eight months ago. However, I am not suggesting that that lessens the pain nor ignorant of the fact that the absence of their father will be a persistently painful fact of life. Do continue to pray for their dear little souls who rest now solely in a Heavenly Father's care.

We went to visit the gravesite today - the children and I. It is a quiet, peaceful, historical site surrounded by fields and many old headstones.

Dying is but getting dressed for God,
Our graves are doorways cut in sod."

~ from Calvin Miller's Symphony in Sand

Saturday, February 24, 2007

It being one week ago today I said my earthly goodbye to my beloved, it seems appropriate to go back to those last days with him, as for many of you there is a gap when I did not write much on the site those days. And I would like to share how God showed His mercies even then.

The beginning of that final week of Vernon's life, he became increasingly uncomfortable. It was difficult for him to put it into words how he felt. When I would gently probe him to describe how he felt physically, he would say he didn't know how to but it was obvious there was a decline in his comfort level. On Monday, though his legs and feet were incredibly swollen, he worked all day on making a wooden towel rack (which is now proudly mounted in our bathroom). That was on his "to-do" list and he was adamant he was going to tackle it that day, whether I thought it a wise investment of his time or not.

By Tuesday, he was feeling noticeably worse. We had talked of going out for Valentines Day but the weather and his condition made that out of the question. Wednesday, then, he spent mostly on the couch, increasingly fatigued. That evening was the very first that he spoke of his longing to leave this earth and complete the journey to his heavenly home. I knew then he really did not feel well. Thursday and Friday found him in a rapid decline of disorientation, weakness and weariness. I learned through this experience that there are levels of comas. By Saturday midday, he was completely oblivious to his surroundings. Through wretchedly hard it is to see a loved one go in this condition, it was merciful of our Father to spare him incredible suffering at the end. We were able to manage his pain and breathing through meds alone, which was a blessing. For months, my heartfelt prayer had been that my children need not see their Daddy in immense prolonged suffering. God answered that prayer.

All day on Saturday, I debated how to handle his passing with the children, not wanting for them to have to endure long, vigilant hours by his bedside, embedding in their tender memories a languishing father. We were incredibly blessed by a family friend from Virginia, an RN who came Saturday morning (I called her early that morning, feeling panic-stricken at the thought of a hospice nurse only stopping several times a day). This dear friend had offered her time for however many days we needed her to be here to help with Vernon's care at the end. After she came, I was able to relax that he was medically being taken care as best as possible. She also was able to monitor him continuously and keep us informed of the progression towards the finality of death.

Our children had been out or away much of the day with cousins at play. So when the time came that the nurse told us the end was near, we called for the children to be brought. My youngest remained puzzled through much of the encounter. Assembled around Vernon where he rested on the chair, the oldest three children were sobbing their hearts out. It was a moment I was not prepared for. I confess that as I struggled to extend my arms to enfold all four of them, I felt the weight of the world on my shoulders as it seemed to me a picture of life to come - one parent simply unable to meet the needs of all my children. I attempted to console both my offspring and reach out to my beloved as he breathed his final breath. My children continued to cry their hearts out (an intimate scene I could never adequately describe); several of them sobbed themselves to sleep right there with their Daddy. God's mercies were there in that, in being bedtime, they were able to be sound asleep, exhausted with grief when the coroner carried his earthly tent away.

The next days were a bit of a blur as we made necessary funeral and burial arrangements. I am so very grateful for the multitude of friends and family who came to show their love and support! The viewing and the funeral were packed with those who came to express their respect for a man whose life I am honored to have shared.

Saturday, February 24, 2007

I do not like to tell people how to pray for I know the Spirit can better lead. Yet many are asking.

Do keep Vernon's parents uplifted to the Father. It is so very hard to have to bury one's child.

Sleep does not come easy for me, thoughts difficult to manage.

The last of my family pulled out this morning. My children had great fun playing with their cousins this week. But admittedly, my pulse races faster at the thought of now having to face life alone as reality will set in. Yet I know it needs faced and the children, I suppose, need some sense of normalcy resumed.

Come, children, let us go!
"Our father is our guide;
And when the way grows steep and dark,
He journeys at our side.
Our spirits He would cheer,
The sunshine of His love
Revives and helps us as we rove,
Ah, blest our lot e'en here!

~ Gerhard Tersteegen, 1697-1769

Sunday, February 25, 2007

Of course it wasn't easy going to church without Daddy for the first time this morning. How Vernon always loved the Lord's Day; now we can envision him basking in the presence of our God, first-hand and every day!

Words from a song we sang in church this morning say it well:

Not all my prayers and sighs and tears
Can bear my awful load.
Thy grace alone, O God...
No strength save that which is divine
Can bear me safely through.

~ Horatius Bonar, 1864

Monday, February 26, 2007

I am unsure whom my oldest daughter has overheard or why this holds a novelty for her, but she has said numerous times to me the past few days: "Mom, you're a widow." I've always thought widow an ugly word - sort of like a windowless world.

New aspects to our fatherless situation that strike me is mail addressed only to me or the now-vacant front seat in the van which requires a new seating arrangement for the children.

God give me wisdom with my children. Not wanting to choose the easiest path, avoid truthfulness or divert grief, but also needing to discern maturity sensitivities. Last night at bedtime Tia raised her arms heavenward and said, "Good night, Daddy." Then tonight I heard the children discussing that Daddy is surely in our midst and can he read our minds?

There were some literal tears slipping into our Cheerios this morning as the absence of our Daddy was sorely felt as we readied ourselves for the first day back to school. Daddy was a vital part to the beginning of our school day. The boys were dreading school but I think tomorrow should be less difficult. Tia, on the other hand, came out with a beaming face this afternoon when I picked them up. Helping them with their homework will be a new chore for me as their Daddy loved to do that with them.

Insomnia seems to be everywhere, judging by the pledges of nighttime intercession sent my way. I am sorry for your loss of slumber but grateful my past several nights have been well. I think grief brings with it a weariness all its own.

Will not the end explain
The crossed endeavor, earnest purpose foiled,
The strange bewilderment of good work spoiled,
The clinging weariness, the inward strain,
Will not the end explain?

Meanwhile He comforteth
Them that are losing patience. 'Tis His way:
But none can write the words they hear Him say
For men to read; only they know He saith
Sweet words, and comforteth.

Not that He doth explain
The mystery that baffleth, but a sense
Husheth the quiet heart, that far, far hence
Lieth a field set thick with golden grain
Wetted in seedling days by many a rain;
The end -- it will explain.

~ Amy Carmichael

Wednesday, February 28, 2007

I was going through my personal journal this morning and came across a prayer entry I had written six weeks before Vernon's death. It does sum it up well...

"Thank you Lord, for Your Word. Thank you for Your mercies which are new every morning. And Lord, right now, even though I can't envision life without my husband, can't imagine a morning worth living without him, God, I place my trust in You that Your mercies will be there, and You will enable me to put one foot in front of the other, and not only that but that you will make my life worth living. Thank you that even through my tears of despair, your grace enables me to not forsake you."

Though I'd rather a day was not just something to get through, I trust my God for future joy in living. I am deeply grateful for my children and especially my preschooler who helps keep me from complete introversion. I miss my husband so rawly the word heart-break needs no defining. And there are times I look at my children in utter despair over their rearing. Please pray for wisdom in parenting as I deal with attitudes and actions no doubt related to their grieving process.

As much of my time the past seven months was spent in caregiving for my beloved, this establishing of a new norm to daily life and activity is difficult to adjust to.

Pray for my children, that they might be able to process their mother's breakdowns at odd moments. Sometimes they simply cry with me, other times they disappear, but most times they just go on about business as usual. There is no need to ask why or what's wrong.

Not sure that this is actually scientifically proven, but a friend of mine shared: "Did you know that they've analyzed tears from folks experiencing grief or sorrow and tears versus from someone cutting an onion and there is a difference? The "sad" tears have toxins in them that represent something our bodies need to be rid of... and the "onion" tears don't."

Pass the tissues, please.

Tears may soothe the wounds they cannot heal. ~ Unknown Author

O Holy Saviour, Friend unseen,
The faint, the weak on thee may lean,
Help me, throughout life's varying scene,
By faith to cling to thee.

~ Charlotte Elliot, 1789-1871

Saturday, March 3, 2007

More milestones passed. Tonight two weeks. Again, some of Vernon's family came and we commemorated by hymn singing.

Jed's first hockey game without Daddy there cheering him on. As I watched our firstborn on the ice, my mind couldn't help going back to the years when I watched Vernon play the game with such ardor.

As I sort through my beloved's clothes, I finger the fabric, memories streaming. My heart swells with love and pride for the man he was. Through the huge lump in my throat, the pain in my chest, I smile with fondness of times gone by, shared moments of life God granted us together - truly a mercy everlasting. How I thank God for the privilege of having known him, having loved him and been loved by him. And how grateful I am for the four precious reminders of that love. And as I sort through his clothes - some will go to bless others in need - some to rags; I thought how symbolic of his life itself - moments for God's glory, other moments one can only view as stepping stones of sanctification.

I marvel at God's mercy in my grief. Though I miss my husband so much it literally hurts, I can sense God's comfort in a quite unexplainable way. And when I think I must ask my husband a question or just want to share something with him, it is God I need now turn to. I am coming to better comprehend the special relationship between a widow and her God.

And God continues to extend His comfort. I was looking at photo albums the other evening which had caused the floodgates to open, both with longing for my husband and with appreciation for all he was, when my six-year old came and gave me this note: "Tia to Shairron. I love you you are nice. I miss are dad and am sheyou do to. it's ok to cry. dont worry I love you and Jesus Loves you to."

Do you think that the infinite God cannot fill and satisfy your heart?
~ Francois De La Mothe Fenelon, 1651-1715

Wednesday, March 7, 2007

In pondering events I've found myself immersed in, I've come to the thought that to ask "Why?" is, in a sense, to deny grace. Rather, I must bow in humility and bask in the fullness of *Him*.

There are plans for an auction to liquidate Vernon's landscape equipment. I can not adequately describe the feelings that emerged as the auctioneers, Vernon's father and I walked through the shed discussing details. I felt my respect for my husband swell. Memories of the man whose sweat and toil provided for the family he cherished. It wasn't hard to remember the strong man he was who toiled in God's earth day after day creating masterpieces out of Creation. God had given Vernon a talent for design and he so enjoyed the challenge and fulfillment of his work.

How are my children doing? A question spoken and unspoken with frequency.

They are little sinners as you and I, with hurting hearts as you and I. Yet I see the Master Sculpture's Hand carving Christ's fullness while applying His sealant of mercy. I experience a bond with my offspring as never before. We share our tears, our joys and our fears. Perhaps my firstborn saw the look of despair upon my features last evening when he came and gave me a kiss and expressed his verbal appreciation for me. The mercy drops yet fall.

We talk of Daddy with frequency and frankness. We pray God enables us to remember more of the Daddy before he was sick and not the Daddy he was when not himself. We rejoice he has reached his ultimate goal - his heart's desire - to be complete in Christ. Yet how we miss the man who gave our lives stability and our hearts joy. We weep into our pillows at night and valiantly try to face the sunshine of the new day with a smile. Grievers on a journey not alone and yet our own. Guided by a new understanding of trust and faith in our Heavenly Father who promises to be our provider and defender.

It seems odd to set the table for just five, and there is a constant vacancy felt in our living room. Bedtime ritual brings its own pain. And often can be heard the comments "I miss Daddy" or "I want Daddy." However God enables us to also breathe a prayer of thanks that Daddy is in heaven. Perhaps there is no better release for one to let a loved one go than to have etched in one's memory the suffering this earthly life afforded.

Long have I viewed, long have I thought,
And held with trembling hand this bitter draught;

'Twas now first to my lips applied;
Nature shrank in, and all my courage died.
But now resolved and firm I'll be,
Since, Lord, 'tis mingled and reached out by Thee.

Since 'tis thy sentence I should part
With the most precious treasure of my heart,
I freely that and more resign;
My heart itself, as its delight is thine.
My little all I give to thee-
Thou gavest a greater gift, thy Son, to me.

~ Octavius Winslow, 1808 -1878

Thursday, March 8, 2007

Written by one who has been there... every time I read this, my tears flow as it expresses it so well... the writer a virtual stranger to me yet willing to bare his heart... we trust it can strengthen another on their journey...

One by one they come to shake my hand, to hug me, to assure me that they are praying for me and my children. I watch with numbness as the chairs are arranged in the auditorium and the church is being returned to normal. I watch as they leave, in couples and in families, they have done all that they could, now they are leaving - Leaving to go back to their lives as usual - but I am alone - usual and normal are gone forever. Our marriage is over, for our family, it will never be the same.

I awake, is this really true? Yes, "today is the first day of the rest of my life", There is a sense of peace that I have never felt before, but it does not compensate for the pain -real pain - like someone were reaching down my throat trying to pull my heart out.

Why God? Do you get some kind of pleasure from taking daddies who are needed so much? There are thousands of fathers who don't know or don't seem to care about their families, why do you take the ones that care so much and work so hard to make a life for them?

Certainly there are many parents better qualified to be single parents than I. Why am I thrust in this place? Kids weren't designed to be raised by only one parent. They need the experience and strength of a father along with the compassion of a mother. Why have my kids been asked - no, they weren't asked - they were just suddenly without their father. How can any good be accomplished by this tragedy?

Have I done something to deserve this? Has this come because of my ungratefulness, my foolishness, some slip of the tongue or thought? Is this all my fault? Has my faith failed?

I watch my children suffer in silence. I long for the proper words to heal their pain quickly but I have none. I observe that the slightest bump or scratch can bring an almost unstoppable flood of tears and crying. I see them try to be brave for my sake. We huddle together; subdued, afraid, devastated. Will this pain ever find relief? Will there ever again be life with some meaningful purpose other than making it through the day physically, mentally and emotionally intact?

Who will be my counselor? Who will tell me when I need to be more firm or more understanding? Who will be there to comfort my children when I am not in an emotional state to do it? Who will fill the gaps in my schedule when I cannot be there for them? God, the questions go on and on. I must stop and wait at your feet. You allow me to shout questions but your answers are sometimes withheld because I cannot understand them. Either I'm not ready for your answers or they are not comprehendible by humans.

God, I trust you. I trust you with my whole heart. I trust as I have never trusted before because I have never before been in a place where I have had so little control. Lord, if I wait on you in the stillness I can feel your arms around me. They are strong arms - I feel loved by you. God, I want to pass on that love and security to my children, but sometimes I need it all myself.

Sometimes I can't comfort them because of my own pain. You will need to be their daddy. You will need to be there personally for them and sometimes send someone to be their daddy for a day, or a week, or just an evening.

Lord, I know you do nothing without careful planning. I know that my healing and the healing of my children have not been left to chance. I know that your provision for us spiritually, physically and emotionally have not been cast to the wind, nor have you deserted me to figure it all out for myself. We are in the center of your divine plan but this is one of the times when being in your will is not comfortable or easy. However, there is a joy unspeakable that permeates our lives and it is only because you are our sustainer as you promised.

God, there are just a few thing that I ask - give me wisdom and discernment. Help me identify self-pity - it keeps me from healing. Help me to identify grief - it is an essential part of healing. Help me to accept the well meant if not so well spoken words of those who want to offer encouragement, but aren't sure how (how could they know - I often don't know what it would take to encourage me either). Protect me from the martyr complex - it leads to a life of existing. Help me to know when I'm not making time for me - if I don't, my kids get shortchanged too. Give me a sense of balance. Protect me from guilt - I know we did the best we knew how.

God, I believe you made every provision for our healing before this all began. We reach out to you and claim and accept those provisions.

Help us to know with certainty that through the tears and pain we are overcomers through Him that loved us and purchased us with His own blood.

Jesus, take this burden and carry it for me.

~ "The Heart Cry of the Single Parent" by Sam Beiler

Wednesday, March 14, 2007

We all know the question "How are you?" to a griever sounds

so frustratingly trite. I assure you the appropriate answer is no easier.

Life goes on. More landmarks passed. I wonder when I will stop thinking about "firsts" without Vernon. It seems unbelievable to me that it is only going on four weeks since his passing; it feels like so much longer. The words of the old hymn sum it up well: "Oh to grace how great a debtor, daily I'm constrained to be!" Were it not for God's grace and mercy, I would be forever plunged into a deep abyss. Grace aside, I miss my husband so much at times I literally ache and tears run furiously. Mercy afforded, I wrestle with despair at meeting the needs of my children: emotional, spiritual and physical needs; seemingly insatiable and quadrupled.

At times the precipice seems to be irresistibly drawing me to its edge. My vain efforts at denying memories, keeping up with the constant demand for activity, stifling torrents of tears, panicking at the thought of entering the black hole I found myself in after the loss of my Mother - prostrate before the Father yet seemingly no sun in sight. Though I have The Son, I want more. I don't want to increase my children's pain by exposing them to the anxiety of seeing a mom who cannot cope. I want to be strong, tell me wherein weakness is a positive attribute? - save I know - I know - then "He will be strong." But God, why must you use your staff to pull me back up? I want to walk upright.

And were I not to apply literally Jesus' words about not fearing for the morrow, or to effectively believe that God's grace will be sufficient for the day and claim His promise that He will not give me more than I can bear, the abyss looms nearer. Were I not to take captive those thoughts that threaten to plunge me over the edge, ah - but the Shepherd readies His staff.

Jesus deals very gently with those who find the cross heavy. He sympathizes, for He knows what it means to suffer. He sank under His own cross, and had to be helped with it by a passer-by on the way to Calvary.

~ J. R. Miller

'Daughter, take up thy cross and follow me',
I hear, O Master, and would follow still,
Did not my frame, grown weaker than my will,
Because my long-borne cross weighs heavily,
Most helpless sinks when I would most obey;
But Thou that in Gethsemane did pray
The cup might pass, if such His will might be,
Till Thou wast over-worn in agony,
And so didst sing, exhausted on the way
To Calvary, till they raised the cross from Thee-
Thou wilt not chide if for a while at length
Weakened by anxious vigil, wrestling, loss,
Sinking, and finding none to raise my cross,
I lie where fallen, and wait returning strength.

~ Unknown Author

Thursday, March 15, 2007

In memory of Vernon, because it was this blessed assurance that he clung to and those who knew him well knew his passion for this doctrine...

Genuine holiness will yield you a heaven hereafter; but genuine assurance will yield you a heaven here. He who has holiness and knows it, shall have two heavens--a heaven of joy, comfort, peace, contentment, and assurance here--and a heaven of happiness and blessedness hereafter.

Genuine assurance will be a spring of joy and comfort in you. It will make heavy afflictions light, long afflictions short, and bitter afflictions sweet. It will make you frequent, fervent, constant, and abundant in the work of the Lord. It will strengthen your faith, raise your hope, inflame your love, increase your patience, and brighten your zeal. It will make every mercy sweet, every duty sweet, every ordinance sweet, and every providence sweet. It will rid you of all your sinful fears and cares. It will give you ease under every burden, and make death more desirable than life. It will make you more strong to resist temptation, more victorious over opposition, and more silent in every difficult condition.

Well, remember this--next to a man's being saved, it is the greatest mercy in this world--to know that he is saved.

~ "Genuine Assurance" by Thomas Brooks, 1662

Saturday, March 17, 2007

*Oh tell me, some one, if you will
Am I awake or dreaming still?*

~ The Adventures of Bobby Raccoon

Today marks the one-month anniversary since God called Vernon home. It's not the best of days. Need I say more.

*For you today, I Am.
I hear your heart, I know your soul.
I see the great, unfettered whole-
But you, my child, cannot unroll
Tomorrow.*

For you today, I Am.
Your fears and doubts of what will be-
Your dreams and longings give to Me.
My child, I gently oversee
Tomorrow.

For you today, I Am.
I Am in happy days, and gray-
I Am where'er your path will lay.
But child, I'm only in today-
Lay down tomorrow!

For you today, I Am.
The past is mine to understand.
I hold tomorrow in My hand.
All these I gently carry and
I'll lead you.

~ Unknown Author

Wednesday, March 21, 2007

As I mourn in my vast void, the pain-filled "'why's?'" plague and threaten to consume. God deals with my wrestling gently. He has sent these reminders...

Whenever we may wander in uncertainty through intricate windings, we must contemplate with eyes of faith, the secret providence of God which governs us and our affairs and leads us to unexpected results.

~ John Calvin, 1509 - 1564

Not yet thou knowest what I do
Within thine own weak breast,
To mould thee to My image true,
And fit thee for My rest.
But yield thee to My loving skill;
The veiled work of grace,
From day to day progressing still,
It is not thine to trace.

~ Frances R. Havergal, 1836-1879

He writes in characters too grand
For our short sight to understand;
We catch but broken strokes, and try
To fathom all the mystery
Of withered hopes, of death, or life,
The endless way, the useless strife,-
But there, with larger, clearer sight,
We shall see this - His way was right.

~ Unknown Author

Friday, March 23, 2007

No need to show up at my door tomorrow with roses or a prescription to treat depression. I know from whom my afflictions come; I know who holds me in His all-sufficient Hands. But I also know that this time is dark and this time is hard. And He allows me, in my heart-wrenching pain, to express my honest thoughts.

Today is mine. Tomorrow is none of my business. ~ Elizabeth Elliot

Sunday, March 25, 2007

Thy grace is my consolation. ~ Gotthold

If I could sum up my thoughts in one line, perhaps that would be it. Despite the pain-filled days and sorrow-filled nights, God enables me to keep my eyes on Him and His unfailing grace.

I must express gratitude for the hundreds of cards and emails I receive. How I wish I could personally respond to each one. They mean so very much! Some come from dear people I don't even know. Some share part of their journey with me and how I cherish those. Some bring a lump to my throat, tears to my eyes, but all buoy my faith. The promise of continued prayers a salve to my soul. The generosity of givers humbly heartening. All are mercy drops.

Other mercy drops this morning include the bright sun on the horizon, the birds singing in the trees, the promise of spring, and more so the thought of my eternal home with both my beloved and my Saviour and God.

God is the master of the scenes; we must not choose which part we shall act; it concerns us only to be careful that we do it well, always saying, 'If this please God, let it be as it is. ~ Bishop Taylor

Tuesday, March 27, 2007

As I sat in church and heard the pastor say how one's mate is your best spiritual friend, I wanted to scream, "You have no idea how I feel like an amputee!" I miss my husband intensely in the early mornings. It was when we communed with our Lord together. And drinking a latte for one just isn't the same. Friends and family are wonderful and I am so well cared for. But to an extent, grief is one's own battlefield. Activity is a band-aid but there's always home to come back to or the reality that hits when the last one goes out the door. There is just always that loss of the one who should be there, the void that can't be filled. The empty chair, the empty bed, the empty pew, the empty everything.

I never knew grief could be so all-consuming. I've never known the sharpness of such loss. There are times I want to retreat under the covers of "no memories" and never come out. Never come out and feel the pang of loneliness, the stab of despair, the blanket of depression, the bottomless ache of grief. I wonder when will the wound stop rubbing raw? When will I stop missing my husband so much it physically hurts? I wonder when life will become something to enjoy? When will my eldest son and I no longer need to stifle resentment when tackling jobs that require a father? Will my preschooler always include Daddy in her stick figure family pictures? When will I stop wincing at how easily the word "death" or "dying" slip off of tongues - the speaker innocent of the darts? When will life resume a semblance of meaning and order without the leader and stability of our home? When will my son, much like his father, stop expressing his emotions of loss through angry outbursts? When will my daughter, who takes life so seriously, stop recollecting stories of Daddy when, in his suffering, he exhibited behavior not typical of our Daddy?

When will I not despair over raising these children alone?

When will everywhere I look not remind me of the man who should be there? When will I stop feeling sorry for myself? When will we stop going through so many tissues?

Sigh.

Perhaps, like Job, I should keep silent or perhaps, like David, I may continue to cry out the God who hears me and measures my tears. It is by no means that I do not yet hold to the truths that have sustained me the past eight months. God is still good, faithful and able and I can say that with my whole soul, body, strength, and mind. I do not doubt His ability, His attributes or anything about His ways I may not presently appreciate. Nevertheless, in all honesty, what weighs heaviest on me now is the dark and the drear; the dungeon. I continue to trust wholeheartedly in His goodness and am content in where He has me. Because I am content, however, does not mean I am enjoying it, if that makes any sense or is allowable. But I will "wait for the Lord; be strong and take heart and wait for the Lord" (Psalms 27:14 NIV) because He hath promised: "The Lord gives strength to His people; the Lord blesses His people with peace." (Psalms 29:11 NIV)

Blessed God! Thou has often taught us lessons in the shade we should never have learned in the sunshine.
~ James Harington Evans, 1785-1849

Tuesday, March 27, 2007

"And a little child shall lead them." (Isaiah 11:6 KJV) Well, who can remain gloomy when the spring sun shines brightly and your four-year old requires you to sing with her "Great Is Thy Faithfulness", repeatedly, for fifteen minutes straight!

The waves are many, and the storm is furious; but I fear not to be drowned, for I stand upon a Rock. ~ Chrysostom, 349 – 407

Thursday, March 29, 2007

To all my fellow sailors with storms of their own...

Thy God hath sent forth strength for thee. (Psalm 68:28)

I am tired, Lord: let me furl my sail,
I hear thro' the mists how the sad waves wail,
My heart is quailing, and sick with fear,
Ask me no more on yon course to steer.

"Child, take this word again for Me;
As thy days, so shall they strength be."

Lord, the storm is o'er - we have ridden it well,
Through all its tossing no harm befell,
'Twas Thine hand upon the helm, I know
But the track is so lonely whereon we go!

For the lonely hour, child, trust in Me;
As they days, so shall they strength be;

The canvas is torn, and the rigging rent,
While I see the white sails gleam content
'Neath the golden light on a sheltered bay;
Let me drop my anchor there, Lord, I pray.

Child, thou must leave the choice to Me;
As thy days, so shall they strength be;

Lord, the night is coming - I fear, I fear!
The roar of the breakers is drawing near.
And I cannot turn my bark aside;

These Clouds We So Much Dread

Now must I perish at eventide?

They shall never perish who trust in Me;
As thy days, so they strength shall be;

The billows are past and the harbour won -
We saw in the gleam of the setting sun,
The waters of peace that bark enfold,
And bear it afar into joys untold,

Now heart, be strong to ride life's sea,
As thy days, so shall thy strength be.

~ The Twilight Hour

Tuesday, April 3, 2007

I shock myself sometimes, not only at my thoughts but also at words that come out of my mouth…

This morning as I felt those annoying tears begin to flow again and I reached for the tissue box in disgust, the words "good grief" slipped out of my mouth - then the irony of it struck me. And I have a small, potted dahlia on my windowsill which requires daily attention lest it wilt. I returned home from this past weekend away to find its blooms completely drooped and distraught.. As I nursed it back to joy, I shocked myself this morning as I heard myself say to it, "It's ok, sweetheart, I know how hard it is to get back up." How reminded I am of my needing to receive my daily sustenance in my God.

My mother's birth date approaches. I wonder, was she here, what words of comfort and counsel she might give. Then I must smile as I imagine her and my husband worshiping before the throne in their cancer-free beings.

Sometimes when my children are fighting or the din is absurd, I struggle with just wanting to turn up some loud music and drown them out. Oh, to not choose the easy road with them since I obviously can't simply wait till Daddy comes home and let him deal with a discipline issue or even ask his advice. Many a time I close my eyes and plead for the wisdom of Solomon.

I spent the weekend at a ladies' retreat with our former church. There were six ladies who spoke sharing their paths God hath led them on, and what difficult paths they are. Some have known the sorrow of losing a husband, some the sorrow of losing a child, some the sorrow of living a lifetime with a handicapped child, some shared of the heartbreak of alcoholism, of living with depression, of a husband's unfaithfulness which resulted in the end of their marriage. All have needed to rely on God's sustenance and attested to His mercies, though times are still not easy. Children living astray due to damage done. Some of my "how long" and other questions that I asked did not receive the answers I would've liked to have heard. Oh, if we could only accept that most of our stories we will never see the '"happily ever after" here on this sin-stricken earth.

Cast thy burden upon the Lord, and He shall sustain thee.
~ Psalms 55:22 KJV

It is by an act of simple, prayerful faith we transfer our cares and anxieties, our sorrows and our needs, to the Lord. Jesus invites you come and lean upon Him, and to lean with all your might upon that arm that balances the universe, and upon that bosom that bled for you upon the soldiers spear! But you doubtingly ask, 'Is the Lord able to do this thing for me?' And thus, while you are debating a matter about which there is not the shadow of a shade of doubt, the burden is crushing your gentle spirit to the dust. And all the while Jesus stands at your side and lovingly says, 'Cast your burden upon me and I will sustain you. I am God Almighty. I bore the load of your sin and condemnation up the steep of Calvary, and the same power of omnipotence, and the same strength of love that bore it all for you then, is prepared to bear your need and sorrow now. Roll it all upon Me! Child of my Love! Lean hard! Let Me feel the pressure of your care. I know your burden, child! I shaped it -- I poised it in My own hand and made no proportion of its weight to your unaided strength. For even as I laid it on, I said I shall be near, and while she leans on Me this burden shall be Mine, not hers. So shall I keep My child within the encircling arms of My own love, Here lay it down! Do not fear to impose it on a shoulder which upholds the government of worlds! Yet closer come! You are not near enough! I would embrace your burden , so I might feel My child reposing on My breast. You love me! I know it. Doubt not, then. But, loving me, lean hard!

~ "Lean Hard" by Octavius Winslow, 1808-1878

Wednesday, April 4, 2007

The children and I reminisce (well, they reluctantly oblige my insistence) of life even one short year ago when we still had a Daddy strong and able; a Daddy with smiling eyes and an unequaled joy in his children. The more recent memories, like weeds threaten to choke out the old. One of my children said to me last night, "I don't cry when I remember the good times, I cry when I remember the bad." We wept together, my heart aching at the hurt this child owns. I become enraged at the cruel robber cancer is and the sin it represents.

These past few days have been gloriously spring-like. Yet I walk through my gardens that so personify Vernon with the unbidden phrase of "I hate life" overpowering my thoughts. I feel the sunshine but it doesn't penetrate. I come up the steps and into a house so desolate. I look at life with no hope of joy in the morrow. I am shocked by the intensity of my loneliness, by the bleak vacancy a life can create by its absence, startled by the vehemence of the love I feel for the man no longer mine to have and to hold.

Yet through the blear, God remains my Stronghold, my hope of Glory. I cling to His promise of eternity unmarred by this sin-stained earth.

Question & Answer One in the Heidelberg Catechism (1576) was dear to Vernon and he had our family memorize it in the month prior to his death... "What is your only comfort in life and in death? That I am not my own, but belong - body and soul, in life and in death - to my faithful Savior Jesus Christ."

Monday, April 9, 2007

How can one begin to describe the emotions that accompany an auction where the tools of the trade that were the toil and joy of my husband had a value put on them by the highest bidder? To know that I'll never again hear his work truck come rattling in the lane or see him painstakingly laboring over a seeding or stone project brings a full and unequaled force of sadness. But the softening of the sharpness of the loss came from family and friends who showed their support through their presence and the extensive volume of physical labor involved both in behind the scenes work and auction prep. The proceeds from the business portion of the auction exceeded what my husband ever felt it was worth. It was obvious that the Lord's hand of blessing was being displayed.

Family and friends had also organized a benefit auction and the generosity of the donors and buyers resulted in a sum that also exceeded expectations. I could never adequately thank all who participated in that, so please accept this as my feeble effort. I am forever indebted to my God's goodness demonstrated through His people.

My God, how endless is Thy love!
Thy gifts are every evening new,
And morning mercies from above
Gently distill like early dew.

I yield my powers to Thy command,
To Thee I consecrate my days;
Perpetual blessings from Thine hand
Demand perpetual songs of praise.

~ Isaac Watts 1674-1748

Friday, April 13, 2007

Never having been one to whom decisions came easy, I find having half of me - and especially the authoritative half - missing leaves an abysmal void. Many times I cry out to God to fulfill His promise to be my Heavenly Husband. I plead for Him to impart wisdom to me on many a matter. Whether it's wisdom in a battle with my adolescent son over a controversial computer game, or wisdom in the purchase of a lawnmower, or wisdom in leading my children in their spiritual training, or wisdom in financial matters. How I miss my strong, level-headed husband. The counsel of godly friends is invaluable, yet it is to God to whom I am ultimately accountable in all matters great or small, and the burden seems ever-present.

I alternate between amusement and alarm at my children's display of their grieving process. One plays at grave digging, burying sticks and placing flowers on top. One said last night they wish Daddy had a walkie-talkie in heaven so that he could tell them what God looks like. One talks to themselves with a picture of Daddy in their hand as if he were speaking to them.

The feeling of surrealness, that this is all a bad dream I will yet awaken from, is rapidly fading. I feel my days merging from a prevailing sense of despondency to rather a deep sadness. Tears still flow readily but there is a subtle change in their meaning. I look at pictures of my beloved and feel my heart wrench at the love I feel for the man and the agony of my loneliness, yet I am increasingly able to thank God for the privilege of the past. I feel a certain healing slowly beginning, the numbing, gut-wrenching pain merging to an immeasurable sadness.

No hope of rest in aught beside,
No beauty, Lord, I see;
But seek the rest, the peace, the joy,
That dwells, my God, with thee.

~ Unknown Author

Saturday, April 14, 2007

Obviously the need for updates on Vernon's health has expired. Why I continue to write on the site is a question I sometimes ask myself. I guess the answer is that it keeps my friends informed of my level of sanity. All that to say, I understand if the vast majority of you stop returning to the journal. What I have to say is not inspirational. It is my bare facts of my life, the ups and downs of my days as they are now meted out to me. I don't pretend to be coping well, to have any of the answers (as if there were any). I am simply a sinner saved by grace; hurting like a puppy, yet clinging to my Heavenly Father's hand.

Weekends have become a time of much mixed emotions. I look forward to the children being off school, not only for their presence but for the laxness in schedule it brings. Yet it seems the weekends are when the absence of a husband and father are most felt. Last week when my brother's family was here, he was telling the story about Elijah, the widow and the oil, and he used the word "family" to describe the widow and her son. My young nephew innocently insisted that they were *not* a family as there was no father. As hard as I want to argue that it isn't so, the reality of the bite is deep. We may yet be a family but how it feels fragmented and fragile. Weekends used to be a time of togetherness; we were happiest home alone. I now find myself wanting to fill up those vacancies and I don't want it to be that way. I don't want to evade the solitariness I've always valued or for my home to be a place of discontentment.

I worked out in the flowerbeds this morning until I became so disheartened by the weeds and the memories. Overwhelmed with the amount of work and engulfed with the memories and the loss of the man that should be by my side (and created all this work!), I came in frustrated and adamant that I do not want to live at this place another spring. The work and memories are too overpowering.

Crying is all right in its way while it lasts. But you have to stop sooner or later, and then you still have to decide what to do. ~ C.S. Lewis

Sunday, April 15, 2007

Last evening the children and I considered the likelihood of many robins in heaven. This morning we awoke to a steady deluge of rain, also to a child too sick to venture out to Lord's Day worship.

I heard a robin singing in the rain,
Its bird-soul pleading low. Again, again
It called to those sore-spent with Life's dull sting
To open their soul-windows to the Spring.
Surely it seemed those vibrant notes might lend
Fresh courage; my tired heart defend
'Gainst utter numbness. Yet all sound
First touched my senses, sorrow-bound, in vain,
E'en as the tranquil cadence of the rain
Upon a home deserted, lone, remote.
And then there fell one low, pulsating note,
That jarred a slumbering hurt and freshly smote
My soul, awoke the old insistent pain; -
New consciousness and heart to fight again.

~ Mary Baldwin

Monday, April 16, 2007

My Monday Morning…

I don't remember signing up for this. But let me start from the beginning. I awoke this morning to a soft light outside - an immediate cause for alarm - which, sure enough, a quick check of my cell phone confirmed the alarm was off. As I arose and looked outside, I was not prepared for the second shock. Four inches of snow covered everything. Our poor rooster's muffled crow was coming from inside the ice-laden bush where they roost. I could barely see patches of black feathers. Then I notice the chill in the house. Ah yes, electric off, this now means no heat or water. Of course, that would also equate to no brushing teeth, flushing toilets and worst of all *no coffee*. I sat and pondered how I might come up with some form of hot water. I even entertained the idea of starting a campfire outside (albeit that thought was brief). Made some phone calls to discover that just eight miles to our east, there was no snow, so school was on schedule for everyone else.

As my children started crawling out of their cozy beds and three of us are snuggled up with multiple blankets, the youngest vomits on everything (do remember there is no water to wash up with). Sigh. When the electricity came back on (praise God! I am not a good "rough it" camper), the children and I rush around getting washed, dressed, and all the good Monday morning school stuff.

Might I add my eldest had the worst of attitudes, especially when asked the absurd (to him) request that he go out and shovel at least the large hunks of snow off the driveway nearest the road in hopes that we might pummel our way up and out. Meanwhile, I am fighting tears of self-pity, myself, as I am clearing what seems like half a foot of snow off the van which I had unwisely parked outside last night (innocent of this brewing storm). Had a conversation with my son, I am ashamed to admit with voices raised, about the pure suckiness of our situation in not having a dad but couldn't we at least make the best of our new tasks with appropriate attitudes (this while standing under a pine tree that is dropping buckets of wet snow and ice on us with wind howling viciously about). Oh, forgot to mention that, by now, I am completely stuck in my driveway after having made several phone calls to my father-in-law who assured me I would be able to get out. So, I called him once again to the rescue. After his failed attempts, he decides to take the children himself (seeing as he is wisely parked up on the road), they are now two hours late and of course elated (not) that Grandpa is taking them instead of Mom.

So, here I am finally with computer access, opening my inbox to dozens of new e-mails. Good morning to you. Sorry to disappoint you further about my ungodliness. I do realize there are starving children in Africa, I do realize there are wars going on, I do realize that I have been spoiled in the past by a wonderful man who spared me from some of what I must now deal with alone. I also "know that all things work together for good to them that love God." (Romans 8:28 KJV) Now if only I would stop trying to figure out what that good could be!

Monday, April 16, 2007

My Monday Afternoon Sequel…

Well, perhaps I should have just stayed in bed today. Halfway to school this afternoon, I begin to realize that my need to have a tight grip on the wheel is more than just a strong wind and that thumping sound that is getting louder is more than large chunks of wet snow sliding off my van. Praise God that the final straw (or should I say thud) occurred right near a car dealership with a service area. When I breathlessly ran in the door (I was running late to pick up school children), the pitying look I received from the young man who was looking out the window confirmed my suspicion that my predicament was indeed not good. He graciously led me to the service area where they handed me the keys to a "rental" car and I was off within minutes. Bear in mind I'd never been to this place before but I *like* them now! I snatched their card off the counter as I ran out and later read interestingly enough that their motto is: "All About *Trust*" - to that I must agree!

I needed to get my boys to an appointment ten minutes after school, so the race was on. Alas, a call to my cell from the car place saying the damage is worse than expected and they will need to order a tire and will not be able to complete it until tomorrow and regretfully they need their car back before then. Thank God for dear new friends who truly go the second mile. The doctor who was seeing the boys and heard my cell phone conversation offered their extra vehicle. So, with a creative criss-crossing of the county and the sacrifice of his dear wife's time, I returned the rental car and am appreciatively using their van. Then off it was to music lessons and a mom who sat numbly sipping coffee in a McDonalds while watching her children in the outdoor play land in 40 degrees with blustery winds.

I am home now, still waiting on things to "work together for good."

Tuesday, April 17, 2007

Today marks two months since God called Vernon home. My darling four-year old could not have said it better this morning as she voiced this sentiment: "We still need Daddy."

> *'I can't!' despairingly I cried!*
> *This gentle whisper sounded at my side,*
> *'Of course not, child, Thou wast not fashioned so,*
> *But I, thy Father, can and will. I know*
> *Thy weakness, all thy longing see,*
> *And I am always strong to strengthen thee.'*

~ Mary O'Hara, 1885-1980

Thursday, April 19, 2007

The children and I, along with one of my nieces, are traveling to Ohio for a wedding this weekend. Many have expressed concern how I will emotionally handle a wedding alone, so soon after my beloved's passing. However, she is too good of a friend to miss it and her family quite dear to me. And I am pleased that my eldest son agreed to be my escort to the wedding.

Do not look at your fatherless children with an expression of deep grief. They are more than ever the Lord's children now - the heritage of Him who drew the little children towards Him and blessed them. Neither should you fear the heavy burden of cares, the difficulties that may arise, the dangers that may threaten; nor yet your own weakness, your want of wisdom, your short-sightedness, your lack of that strong army which hitherto supported you so faithfully. All your difficulties will pass away like a cloud, and you will find that as your day is so will your strength be. Only keep your eyes fixed upon Jesus, who goeth before you and will clear the way step by step. If a wall should rise, He will make you to leap over it. If a troop should come up, He will make you to run through it. Only keep close to Him, and, weak woman though you be, you will, with your children by your side, run and not be weary, walk and not faint.

~ James Pryor

Monday, April 23, 2007

Thanks for the covering of prayer I felt this past weekend. God extended traveling mercies and the wedding was actually a blessing. I was able to sit through the service, fondly remembering my beloved, and God's grace grants me gratefulness for what I had and not bitterness over what I no longer have. The beauty of young, adoring love was refreshing.

As I mourn the absence of my husband, however, I find myself reflecting more upon the meaning of the union of marriage and the intimacy of that bond of two becoming one. I am deeply disturbed of late at seeing couples throw this treasure aside. Through eyes so filled with tears I cannot even see, I want to shout: "You fools! How can you be so blind?"

I am grieved by husbands who cherish their work or their dreams above the wife of their youth. I am saddened by the indifference or unkindness I see in husbands treating their wives. I am angered by the disharmony of this union that is to be a reflection of Christ and His love for the church. I just want to shake some men and say, "Why don't you love and cherish the help meet God gave you?" I want wives to grasp that her husband, no matter how seemingly unlovable or worthy of respect, has been given to her by the Giver of all good gifts. My heart aches at all the pain I see in so many marriages. I know too well that we have no promise of tomorrows together.

And this day brings yet again the sobering reality of the brevity of life and the loss of a mate. Spring seems to have arrived, yet the sun and the warmth of the day softens only a little the difficult milestones of what we call funerals. Today I grieve with another young widow whose husband's earthly life was also claimed by cancer. Tomorrow it will be with a friend whose elderly father finished his battle with Parkinson's. The reality of our broken bodies and the heavenly home we long for never lets us rest.

It is to be feared that the most of us know not how much glory may be in present grace, nor how much of heaven may be obtained in holiness on the earth. ~ John Owen, 1616-1683

Wednesday, April 25, 2007

Today I sat and wept with a friend hurting over a recent loss, recounting the memory of fresh death yet a raw wound. I stifled moments of resentment at having to redress my own bandage. I told God I didn't ask for this job of being able to truly "mourn with those who mourn." Yet laughter blended with our tears and the recounting of God's mercies was restorative.

Then the delivery of flowers from friends… flowers the reminder of my loss and pain but also my growth and gain.

Tonight it was tacos over another friend's table. I confess when I entered her house, I was irritated by the presence of the wheelchair and all it represented. I wanted to scream at God, "Why can't I get away from this? I got rid of the one at my house, why do I have to see it here? Why does this pain and heartache have to continue?" Then I was struck by the beauty of the picture we made as we sat around their table lustily singing "It Is Well With My Soul." There we were, grievers who had recently buried a daddy and those in the midst of a mother's frustrating degenerative handicapped battle. And blessed I was to commune with a whole family again. Even the fatherly discipline strengthened my soul.

Then came the negative news of test results in yet another friend's cancer growth. I rinsed my dishes with my tears.

Indeed, tears and mercy drops like the rain falling outside truly danced a staccato this day.

We dare not steel ourselves against our trials, running away from the fires where our pruned branches crumble to ashes. For if we escape those flames, we will risk barrenness of soul and will miss out on the beauty that only is born through the ashes of yesterdays grief. ~ Carrie Van Roy

Monday, May 7, 2007

I spent this past weekend laughing and crying with the women who knew and loved Vernon best. Vernon's mom and sisters planned a weekend lakeside retreat in Indiana. My children were farmed out in Lancaster County and I came back refreshed to take up my task once again.

The Hill, though high, I covet to ascend,
The Difficulty will not me offend;
For I perceive the Way to life lies here.
Come, pluck up Heart, let's neither faint nor fear;
Better, though difficult, the Right Way to go,
Than wrong, though easy, where the End is woe.

~ John Bunyan

God has been gently but firmly reminding me that I have been straying from His command of "taking one day at a time." It was that admonishment that kept me sane through the uncertain months of Vernon's illness and all of the unknowns that the future would hold. How true it is that any despair I allow myself now comes from looking past getting through just this day.

Do not be fidgety and restless about what shall come on the morrow. You have enough to do each day, enough of evil to bear each day. You need not make yourself so many trials by fancying what you may have another day. Let that alone; only trust God. ~ F.D. Maurice

Well, some of my weariness has been and is being eased by crews of God's own hands arriving to weed and edge and mulch, and weed and mulch and weed and mulch. I don't think I can sufficiently describe the satisfaction this gives me to look out and not be overwhelmed at all the work. For those of you who've not been to our grounds: suffice it to say, Vernon enjoyed creating flower gardens!

If I had a single flower for every time I think about you, I could walk forever in my garden. ~ Claudia Ghandi

How I miss my man. Countless times in a day, I have the thought of wishing I could share something with Vernon. I see a couple laughing together, her head thrown back in mirth; doubtless joy of the moment, joy of each other. Or when I discover a new theological nugget, how I yearn to discuss it with Vernon. When I drive over a freshly paved stretch of road we traveled frequently, I remember the uncomfortableness those previous bumps used to cause him and I wish he could feel it now. When I sit on my deck steps in the fresh spring air, how I wish he were sitting there with me. I miss the bouquets of buds he used to bring me from spring pruning jobs. I miss cooking a meal for his hearty appetite to be my thanks. There isn't much that doesn't bring a remembrance of the man to whom I pledged my life and love to.

You cannot study pleasure in the moment of nuptial embrace, nor repentance while repenting, nor analyze the nature of humor while roaring with laughter. But when else can you really know these things? 'If only my toothache would stop, I could write another chapter about pain.' But once it stops, what do I know about pain? ~ C.S. Lewis

Tuesday, May 8, 2007

A game of Simon Says gone awry, a screaming four-year old with blood seemingly everywhere, three other scared children, and a mom who has never had to deal with something like this before. Thanking God tonight for my husband's parents who live just across the field and are such ready helpers. Grandma stayed with the other children while Grandpa drove Kezia & I to our family doctor who, thankfully, does stitches in his office after hours.

If death my friend and me divide,
Thou dost not, Lord, my sorrow chide,
Or frown my tears to see;
Restrained from passionate excess,
Thou bidst me mourn in calm distress
For them that rest in thee.

I feel a strong immortal hope,
Which bears my mournful spirit up beneath its mountain load;
Redeemed from death, and grief, and pain,
I soon shall find my friend again
Within the arms of God.

Pass a few fleeting moments more
And death the blessing shall restore
Which death has snatched away;
For me thou wilt the summons send,
And give me back my parted friend
In that eternal day.

~ "If Death My Friend and Me Divide" by Charles Wesley

Thursday, May 10, 2007

Kez's forehead seems to be mending just fine. Thanks for all the expressed concern.

These Clouds We So Much Dread

So many people I run into this spring tell me how they "need Vernon". None more than I. None more than I. And in ways that are fathoms beyond landscaping or understanding.

Funny how I inspect every white work truck I pass on the road. Is there writing on the door? Do I know those mud flaps? What I'd give to have my man come rattling in the lane again.

Bad theology abounds in our culture today. Heard this in a song today and couldn't quite be sure I heard correctly: "How do you wait for heaven? Who has that much time?" Excuse me?

Busyness seems to have a topical anesthetic effect. Some wonder how I feel about the approaching summer. I would be a fool to deny that I don't look with some dread toward the season that began the nightmare of our life. To think that one long year ago we lived in the innocent ignorance of what would come to alter our lives so drastically.

The children and I talked around the table the other night about our grief and how we were doing with missing Daddy. We all agreed that time has taken some of the edge off. And although I am grateful for the healing that time grants, this brings a sadness all its own. I can't help but wonder if years from now… will there be dust on his pictures? How often will we speak his name? Will this loss feel like our gain? Guess it's all part of the "grief process" (how I've come to detest that term). I don't want to get over it. I want him back!

And as I mourn the loss of the man I no longer have, the reality of the blessing I had increases. Though I in no way mean to canonize the man Vernon was, the truth is that he was a man who sought God and found Him. His heart's desire to love the Lord with all his heart, soul, strength, and mind was lived out in his quest for spiritual understanding, his appreciation for what his Saviour did for him, his adoration of his children, and his perspective on what really mattered in this life.

I recently read a worthwhile book by John Piper and these segments reminded me of Vernon:

> There is something that captures the soul when we see a man of single-minded passion, persevering against all odds, finishing his course no matter the cost.
>
> I suspect that one of the reasons the Puritans are still being read today with so much profit is that their entire experience, unlike ours, was one of persecution and suffering. To our chipper culture this may seem somber at times, but the day you hear that you have cancer, or that your child is blind, or that a mob is coming, you turn away from the light books to the weighty ones that were written on the precipice of eternity where the fragrance of heaven and the stench of hell are both in the air.
>
> There have always been, as there are today, people who try to solve the problem of suffering by denying the Sovereignty of God - that is, the all-ruling providence of God over Satan and over nature and over human hearts. But it is remarkable how many of those who stand by the doctrine of God's sovereignty over suffering have been those who suffered most and who found in the doctrine the most comfort and help.

Monday, May 14, 2007

Another widow once told me that she found her third month to be the hardest. She suspected the prayers of others had lessened or was it just the reality wearing thin? I'm nearly through my third month and I'd have to say the journey is on the decline.

These Clouds We So Much Dread

The only way to cope is to focus on getting through each day and keep my mind off of the long lonely lifetime of tomorrows. And yet grief with its webs of confusion has me one moment reeling in the horrible reality of it all while at other times I feel a strange surrealness. I am simply weary of tears and pain at the most unexpected moments. Like daggers through my heart come these piercing memories. Grief is so tiring in its relentless pursuit of your emotions.

And think not that losing a Daddy has not its serious repercussions in the hearts of my children. I've got one who admits that they don't think God answers prayers. Another confesses they can't get bad thoughts about God out of their mind. God help us, each one.

God is not a deceiver, that He should offer to support us, and then, when we lean upon Him, should slip away from us. ~ St. Augustine, 354-430

Tuesday, May 15, 2007

What is Lancaster County coming to? Another family murdered. The killer on the loose, they tell us to lock our doors. My children hear the news and ask "why?" "Sin" is all I can sigh.

My preschooler is like a leech these days. Constantly desiring to be right where I am. While I recognize her attachment need for what it is, there are times, nonetheless, that it feels suffocating. Yet I cannot help but continue to thank God for the blessing she is; were I not to have her constant presence and demands, I would surely slip into a pit of self-focused despair.

Last night while digging through a closet, I came across some old photos which included precious years with Daddy. I sat there and bawled and my girls who wandered in simply sat and cried with me.

Spent some time around a campfire the other evening with some of Vernon's old friends. My boys begged to hear more stories as we reminisced his younger years. I couldn't help but think how truly Vernon got a lot of living out of life.

I met a woman the other day who, after asking where my husband was and hearing that he had died three months ago, commented incredulously, "But you are smiling?" Of course God's grace was given the credit but I can't help but continue to marvel at what people expect.

And there are those who, try as they might, simply do not understand grief. When I in complete honesty share something of my struggle, I see that blank look in their eyes and the words they offer confirm to me their ignorance - no matter how well intentioned. There are some things one cannot understand, having never gone through.

My children no longer want to go to counseling. They said they'll talk to me. I hope so. I came away from my mini session last night somewhat disturbed (isn't counseling supposed to help you feel better?). She made it sound like my children's and my needs are insurmountable and that we will be dealing with this forever.

Who am I? This or the other?
Am I one person today and tomorrow another?
Am I both at once? A hypocrite before others,
And before myself a contemptible woebegone weakling?
Or is something within me still like a beaten army
Fleeing in disorder from victory already achieved?
Who am I? They mock me, these lonely questions of mine. Whoever I am,
Thou knowest, O God, I am thine!

~ Dietrich Bonhoeffer, 1906-1945

Sunday, May 20, 2007

Tia came running in the house one evening, excitedly bidding me come see what her and Kez had made in their new sandbox. Complete with sticks used for headstone markers and pansies atop two mounds were the graves of their Daddy and Grandma (my Mother). Then later, when the boys took over the box, here she comes with Daddy's grave on the back of a dump truck, moving it for safe-keeping.

Becoming familiar with others' kitchen tables of late; a welcome respite from the bleakness of home and, judging by my children's comments, they welcome the diversion as well.

Doubtful it is a day passes that I don't have the thought expressed so well by Edna Millay: "Life must go on, I forget just why." God gently yet steadily nourishes my soul in remembrance of my many remaining blessings. I cannot help but pray: "Oh God I am so ashamed. I live and breathe your grace and mercy daily and yet how quick to whine and doubt I am. How like the Israelites of old. Forgive, oh God, renew my faith once more in You."

Father! Whate'er of earthly bliss
Thy Sov'reign will denies;
Accepted at Thy throne of grace,
Let this petition rise.

~ Anna Steele

By afflictions, God is spoiling us [i.e., taking away from us] of what otherwise might have spoiled us. When he makes the world too hot for us to hold, we let it go. ~ John Powell

Wednesday, May 23, 2007

For months (to my irritation), my youngest shed not a tear over her deceased father. Now she has taken (sometimes at the most inopportune times) to a lip-quivering, eyes-filling, wavering wail: "I miss Daddy!" Ah, but this is even harder to deal with then the absence of expression.

My boys… it is hard for them to acknowledge their pain yet my one son said of the other recently: "He just doesn't enjoy life." How it shreds my heart to feel so helpless in erasing the ugliness of this fallen world. I can only point them to the cross.

A strange, unanticipated aspect of grief I find myself in is when I am with new friends who didn't know Vernon. It hurts that they don't know the man he was, his passion for Christ, his smiling eyes, all of him I wish they could know and I feel so helpless in describing.

I find myself each new day with a tad bit more of renewed determination. I can either sit home and wish someone would invite me over or I can make an effort. I can either look at a seemingly insurmountable problem with a sigh and wish that someone would come do it for me or I can roll up my own sleeves and apply myself in a way I've never needed to before. I can sit around and weep over what I no longer have or I can get up, thank God for what I had and go smell a peony.

A few nights back, unable to sleep, I spent some hours reading over my past posts from start to finish. I came away awed at the evident mercies of God through this now nearly past year. How quickly I forget His goodness in the midst of the darkness.

For us, - whatever's undergone,
Thou knowest, willest what is done.
Grief may be joy misunderstood;

Only the Good discerns the good.
I trust thee while my days go on.

~ Elizabeth Barrett Browning

Sunday, May 27, 2007

A few days ago when Kez was having another one of her breakdowns of missing Daddy, I in all my practicality asked her what we should do about it. She replied that we should just cry about it.

School is out and with that seems to come summer in full force. I remember, well, last year at this time commenting to some friends how life was relatively peaceful. It was the calm before the storm as our summer was then plunged into one of upheaval. So, take not today nor any loved one for granted; how soon all of life can be rearranged.

The children and I leave tomorrow for ten days to visit family in the midwest. Covet your prayers for traveling mercies; I am accustomed to many hours on the road but the mileage looks long.

I cannot say,
Beneath the pressure of life's cares to-day,
I joy in these;
But I can say
That I had rather walk this rugged way,
If Him it please.

~ S.J. Browning

These Clouds We So Much Dread

No longer forward nor behind
I look in hope or fear;
But, grateful, take the good I find,
The best of now and here.

~ J.G. Whittier

Thursday, June 7, 2007

Our trip is going well, other than the insane numbers at the gas pump. And though my children are seasoned travelers, for the most part, there are times that the invisible line in the back seat becomes the object of heated discussion - or dare I admit physical altercation between the brothers. And nearing nine hours into our trip the first day, my four-year old sighed, "This is the longest day of my life!" We have covered a lot of miles and I am ready to be home. The children are having so much fun, however, that I consented to extend our stay and we now plan to travel home tomorrow. It feels sadly peculiar that there is not much to go home for.

It feels odd to visit family without Vernon; the absence of his presence, his comments, his questions, his laughter, and his playing with the children is sorely felt. It has been nourishing to the soul to spend time with those so dear, both Vernon's family and mine. The children are enjoying water battles, sleeping out and all the fun that cousins are. We have had the privilege of visiting a zoo, an Arboretum, sail boating, paddle boating, feeding baby lambs, multiple ice cream cones, and even more cups of coffee.

I was treated to twenty-four hours at a private retreat center where silence is not only golden but required. It was a beautifully welcome respite as Paul Tillich has aptly said: "Our language has wisely sensed the two sides of being alone. It has created the word loneliness to express the pain of being alone. And it has created the word solitude to express the glory of being alone."

Friday, June 8, 2007

Thankful for all the prayer coverage in travels. Despite construction delays, a navigational error, and running out of gas along the interstate which ended up including a towing, we are home again, home again (though some of the younger set doubted we would ever get here). We were greeted by an ecstatic dog, some fast-growing infant felines and our faithful pair of fowl. The gardens my husband created are a bittersweet welcome in their June splendor. And we keep discovering fresh evidences of blessings throughout the place including a freshly mowed lawn, home improvements and even groceries in the fridge.

The Lord's goodness surrounds us at every moment. I walk through it almost with difficulty, as through thick grass and flowers. ~ R.W. Barbour

Monday, June 11, 2007

"I wish that Daddy didn't die because when I grow up I would want to marry him." Words from my "baby" who will turn five tomorrow. It will be our first birthday to celebrate without Daddy. I press my tear-stained face against hers, her blond hair wisping to my cheek. She was her Daddy's littlest angel, her sweet-natured smile honey for his soul. Oh how my heart aches for this tender child. What does her future hold? How will I ever portray her Daddy's love for her? The joy she gave him in his last months, she will never know.

These Clouds We So Much Dread

In an attempt to both distract ourselves from our loss yet embrace life as we now live it without our earthly anchor, our summer calendar holds more than it ever has. Summer really is hard. Summer was so much about Vernon. Vernon was so much about summer. When we returned from our time away, I realized how much harder it is to be home and face memories of Vernon everywhere. I commented on this to the children and how sad I was. I was shocked when one of them quietly remarked that we could forget Daddy if we stopped talking about him. I recognize this as their attempt to cover their pain and it certainly is not a new concept on avoiding the difficult path grief is, yet it was a dagger to my heart.

For many a rapturous minstrel among the sons of light,
Will say of his sweetest music, 'I learned it in the night.'
And many a rolling anthem that fills the Father's home,
Sobbed out its first rehearsal in the shroud of a darkened room.

~ Unknown Author

Tuesday, June 12, 2007

Allow Me

Allow me to smile
To laugh
To sometimes pretend life doesn't hurt

Allow me to cry
To be alone
To sometimes wallow in my pain

These Clouds We So Much Dread

Allow me to talk about him
Allow me to not mention his name
Allow me in your life
As mine has rearranged

Allow me to alternate
Between the sunshine and the rain
Even though you might not understand me
And I may not seem the same

Allow me to acknowledge my God
And the part He plays in my maze
Allow me not to question His
Eternal Sovereign Ways

Allow me to grieve in my
Own way and time
Allow me to honor my beloved
In my own frame of mind

Allow me into your soul
Beyond your façade
I know you too have heartaches
Together we'll seek God

Don't try to protect me friend
From further pain
Allow me to encourage
Allow me to mend

Saturday, June 16, 2007

The barrage of advertisements in our culture today does not allow one to escape the fact that a Hallmark Holiday approaches. A "Happy Father's Day" card hangs on my refrigerator; Tia, in her typical, no-nonsense manner, thought it not odd to make one for her mother. And when I told my eldest that I was planning to invite Vernon's family to come on Father's Day, he wondered why we would do that since we did not have a father. I told him the other tempting alternative would be to sit home and feel sorry for ourselves all day since we do indeed not have a father. His broad grin in response was a small mercy drop.

O Lord,
who art as the Shadow of a great Rock
in a weary land,
who beholdest Thy weak creatures,
weary of labor, weary of pleasure,
weary of hope deferred, weary of self;
in Thine abundant compassion,
and unutterable tenderness,
bring us, I pray Thee, unto Thy rest.
Amen.

~ Christina G. Rossetti

Monday, June 18, 2007

I wonder…

Am I broken, God?
…broken and glued.
I wonder
Will the seams

Ever stop showing through?

I wonder…
Will life ever hold
The same substance
As days of old?
Will this void I feel
Ever be filled?

I wonder…
Will true healing have come
When I can say
It is good
Thy will was done?

Wednesday, June 20, 2007

I do not claim to appreciate storms and last night brought some of the harshest thunder and lightning I can remember. The crashes and cracks that reverberated through the floor along with the lightning that lit up the sky kept me from much slumber. I spent some time reviewing my life, confessing my sins and pleading God to please take away the storm (I also discovered that it is physically possible to fit only so many frightened children into one's bed). I had to think how God must laugh at man's attempts at fireworks as He put on His majestic show. I shuddered at the thought of having to face the wrath of such a God as this, as it seemed His power and might were in full display. And then… a quiet; a quiet so still and peaceful it seemed surreal. Ah, the calm after the storm. How like our lives, how like our trials. We may be in the storm now but God will not leave us there. There will come a calm after the storm.

*I do not seek to understand that I may believe
But I believe in order to understand.*

~ St. Ansolem of Canterbury, 1034-1109

I want to thank the anonymous friend of my children's father who sent the Father's Day card to them with the most meaningful personal expressions. May God bless you for that blessing.

Thursday, June 21, 2007

I have struggled in my attempts to put into my own words how incredibly meaningful fellowship with others is to me since our loss. To all who have and are granting these mercy drops to my family, I thank you.

Isn't a meal together the most beautiful expression of our desire to be given to each other in our brokenness? The table, the food, the drinks, the words, the stories: Are they not the most intimate ways in which we not only express our desire to give our lives to each other, but also to do this in actuality?
~ Henri J. M. Nouwen

Saturday, June 23, 2007

Today we celebrate Tia's seventh birthday with a lump in our throat. My brown-eyed girl whose eyes twinkle like her father's used to. How her Daddy adored her, his first little princess. Her passion for life and tender conscience made his heart swell with pride. One year ago she sat on his lap and blew out her candles with not a clue that this year there would be no Daddy. So, we celebrate, yet we ache.

My soul is weary with sorrow; strengthen me according to your word.
~ Psalm 119:28

Monday, June 25, 2007

She spoke of those who had walked with her long ago in her garden, and for whose sake, now that they had all gone into the world of light, every flower was doubly dear. Would it be a true proof of loyalty to them is she lived gloomily or despondently because they were away? She spoke of the duty of being ready to welcome happiness as well as to endure pain, and of the strength that endurance wins by being grateful for small daily joys, like the evening light, and the smell of roses, and the singing of birds. She spoke of the faith that rests on the Unseen Wisdom and Love like a child on its mothers breast, and the melting away of doubts in the warmth of an effort to do some good in the world.

~ Henry Van Dyke, 1852 – 1933

Wednesday, June 27, 2007

We reel under the news that Vernon's sister Liz (born one year older than he) has been diagnosed with lymphoma. It hasn't even been a year since Vernon's diagnosis. Though one might want to question "why?", better we make every effort to run the race set before us with the endurance that only God through His Son can give us. Do pray for the family (husband Virgil, seven children) and of course Vernon and Liz's parents - this is a blow while they were yet getting up from the last one.

My flesh and my heart may fail, but God is the strength of my heart and my portion forever. ~ Psalm 73:26 NIV

Friday, June 29, 2007

The silence seems strange as the cock no longer crows early mornings perched outside my window. It was with some sadness we bid adieu to the rooster Vernon affectionately called Russ who had brought alternating amusement, distraction and frustration to my ailing husband. Vernon enjoyed watching him strut about and his early morning crow was sometimes a welcome respite to Vernon's long nights. However this unfortunate fowl had since, as he matured, became a terror to my daughters. I hesitated to separate him from the hen who was his lone harem and I get conflicting counsel about whether chickens are capable of feeling emotions. And although it feels cruel to me to relegate her to a position of widowhood, it mostly feels sad, like one more piece is removed from the scene of life we used to know.

Loss creates a barren present, as if one were sailing on a vast sea of nothingness. Those who suffer loss live suspended between a past for which they long and a future for which they hope. They want to return to the harbor of the familiar past and recover what was lost. Or they want to sail on and discover a meaningful future that promises to bring them life again. Instead they find themselves living in a barren present that is empty of meaning. Memories of the past only remind them of what they have lost; hope for the future only taunts them with an unknown too remote even to imagine.

~ Jerry Sittser

Sunday, July 1, 2007

These Clouds We So Much Dread

"So how is she doing?"
they ask in somber tones.
"She seems to be doing well"
comes the tentative reply.

"She keeps herself busy,
her head is held up high;
she always has a smile
we rarely see her cry."

Let me tell you how "she's" doing
How she walks this path of grief;
how she faces each new morning
with both dread and relief.

She grieves most when she's at home,
aching when she thinks about him,
missing him more than anything.
She cries best when she's alone.

See sees her children suffer,
their silent hurt displayed
in their attitudes and actions
in everyday life and play.

She cries out to her Saviour,
to the God who took him away;
she relies on the Spirit
her Comforter and Stay.

She claims His promise daily
to not give her more than she can bear.

He has promised to sustain her
through every heartache, every care.

And it is a daily struggle
for tomorrow always comes.
She can never borrow grace
for the battle not yet won.

She must come before the Throne
with her heart broken and bare
accepting His new mercies
allotted as her share.

And though the future looks daunting
she remembers Jesus' words:
"Enough trouble has tomorrow
Seek His kingdom first today."

Wednesday, July 4, 2007

You know the story, friend of a friend. Received news this day that throws me to my knees. A young mother with a three little ones and one yet unborn gets the news of widowhood.

She gets the call
toddler on her hip
"He didn't show at work."
Preschooler clinging to her shins
policeman at the door
baby crying in the crib
"There's been an accident, Ma'am."
She feels the life move within her womb

These Clouds We So Much Dread

"He won't be coming home."
Her nightmare has begun.
How will she ever get through
the coming days and years?
What reservoir could ever hold
the fountain of her tears?
Oh, God, though Your ways
we don't begin to understand -
can't comprehend Your plan;
would You hold this dear one now
tight in the palm of Your hand?
Could You in Your goodness
give her strength to stand.

Thursday, July 5, 2007

Spending a great measure of time with Vernon's family of late, and the talk of cancer rolls easier off our tongues. The report on his sister Liz is a stage four Non-Hodgkins Follicular Lymphoma. We wrestle with breathing a sigh of relief or holding our breath. Vernon's only brother who lives in Colorado flew in this week. It has been painfully notable, the interest my girls take in their uncle with his striking resemblance to their daddy.

When the clouds hide the mountains they are as real as in the sunshine; so the promise and the Providence of God are unchanged by the obscurity of our faith, or the difficulties of our position. ~ Charles H. Spurgeon

Saturday, July 7, 2007

Each summer my husband and I shared in the joy of watching our white lilies blossom. Last summer Tia brought a bouquet of them into the hospital and their fragrance was a welcome respite from the pain of being there.

Vernon's casket was also covered with a cascade of white lilies. This summer, I watch them open alone. It hurts more than I can say.

The Lily Blooms Again

In my garden blooms a lily
its pure white fragrance glory bursts
bringing memories of another summer
before life held so many hurts
Having walked now
through the valley
of the shadow
in the seasons that came between
God, could You now cause me
like the lily
to value life again

Sunday, July 8, 2007

It is perhaps dangerous to maintain a friendship with one in mourning. A friend of mine wryly commented to me the other day, when I was confessing having the need to go back to so many people and apologize for my rudeness, how tiresome retracing my steps must become. So can I just say, that to the many I may have missed - I am truly sorry. Grief is no excuse for my irritability. Even my preschooler said to me one day, "Mom, do you know why I was grouchy today? Because I was missing Daddy." One of the frustrating aspects of this grieving process, I suppose. And I am ashamed that, in the midst of all the blessings

God bestows, I can even be grouchy. Yet the inescapably gaping void my husband left in my life is broad and vast.

To my local loyals, you may want to mark your calendars now. My late dearly beloved's birthday was August 14th and I would like to commemorate his love for our Lord by a hymn sing on our lawn that evening. Bring your lawn chair and your love for giving God glory through song. We'll use the song sheets from the funeral.

I was given, through God's creative goodness (awarded by a local radio station), a five-day family vacation package at a beautiful retreat center along the Chesapeake Bay in Maryland. We picked up my cousin Rose at the airport yesterday and we leave for the Cove tonight. We are all excited about this opportunity. God's hand was so clearly in this as I find it not coincidental that the timing falls on the week in July when first this journey began last year. To be able to be separated somewhat from the memories seems helpful.

Tuesday, July 10, 2007

The anniversary approaches of when my grieving process began. From the day of Vernon's first surgery, I lost the man who I had known as my husband. The physical pain he died trying to deny, coupled with the pain his heart knew of not being able to raise the children he had waited so long for and loved so wholly, took its deadly toll. His eyes never fully regained their twinkle, nor his step its spring. His silent and stubborn suffering surpassed any I've ever seen. His passion for our God never waned, however, and his desire to never outlive his love for Him was granted. Our roles changed, as only those of you who have been a caregiver to a spouse can understand. God was good, though, in many ways; notably in the spiritual intimacy He granted between my beloved and me as we clung to Him together. Yet the journey was bitterly hard and costly in ways I have not shared. There were portions of the journey that we truly walked alone. There were struggles and battles that were never shown to you. For even in the bitter trials, dignity must be preserved. And there are parts of the untold journey yet a fresh wound.

Six weeks after Vernon's diagnosis, when I began the Caring Bridge site and wrote the opening for the My Story page, I certainly never realized how apt the words "life as we knew it ended that day" would become. God is indeed merciful in sparing us more than we can handle with the knowledge of what a tomorrow may bring.

What has been posted in the particularly painful last year of my life, I trust has proved to somehow give you glimpses of God's grace. Had I known in the beginning the vast amount of grace I would need to journey through this past year after my husband was first diagnosed with his terminal illness, I surely would have collapsed beneath the load. It is for this reason the verse which tells us God gives us grace apportioned to our needs of each day alone has taken on a vastly monumental meaning in my daily existence. I pray God would not soon let me forget the lessons learned through the grace of this past year.

Living in this cyber glass house has not been easy. Many a time I cringed as an unknown audience witnessed our humanness for what it really was. It was not without wrestling with God that I posted some of these journal entries, especially those of such a deeply personal nature. Do I not find it disconcerting having a stranger come up to me and tell me they feel like they know me? Do I not shudder at the thought of what some will think when they read the behind-the-scenes struggles? Yet I must continuously return to the Westminster Shorter Catechism

Question and Answer Number One and, if indeed my chief end in life is to glorify God, does not self and my comfort level need to take a back seat? And thus it is I have offered to you my offering to Him in sharing this past year's grace. My prayer would be that you would see His grace, you would long for His grace, you would embrace and experience His grace. And I believe man's chief end was, in some small way, realized, and we together endeavor to fulfill the latter portion of the statement: to glorify Him and enjoy Him forever.

You have journeyed with us through the thick and the thin. You have prayed, you have cared, you have showed Christ's love in ways I could've never imagined or hoped for. Priceless to me are the prayers and the words of encouragement bred through this site. It is your prayers that aid my clinging to our God Who won't let me go. And while this site was originally designed to update you on Vernon's health, it seems to have now evolved into a mourner's journey towards healing.

So the sun continues to rise and the sun continues to set each day on this household of mourners. And the contrast of the hues waxes and wanes with each new day. The children and I continue to reminisce about the man who was the essence of our days and we strive to squeeze meaning and joy out of the road ahead. We will be more than okay; of that I am confident. And though I wouldn't have chosen this path, I do not waver in the firm belief of Vernon's that "God is Good, God is Able, and God is Faithful."

Our griefs cannot mar the melody of our praise; they are simply the bass notes of our life song: To God Be The Glory. ~ C.H. Spurgeon

To grieve is to allow our losses to tear apart feelings of security and safety and lead us to the painful truth of our brokenness. ~ Henri Nouwen

Tuesday, July 17, 2007

    One year ago today
    the surgeon took his knife
    and with his cutting and his scraping
    confirmed the cancer
    that would claim
    more than my husband's life.

    And from that day onward
    as the anesthesia of the numbness
    wore away
    the reality of the pain
    remains with us today.

    Some days it seems a scab has formed -
    the next it's oozing raw.
    When will the Master Surgeon
    lay His scalpel down
    and the memory
    of this incision
    remain only as a scar?

Wednesday, August 1, 2007

    What does this mourner's journey look like?

    It is tears sliding down my cheeks as I hold my daughter missing her daddy and she remarks that her kitten doesn't have a daddy either.

    It is watching my children listen to a sermon on heaven with rapt attention.

It is recollecting with my children the memories that hurt too much representing a missing part of Daddy in our lives.

It is one day wanting to yank those white lilies right out by their roots because they are here and he is not, and then the next day wishing their fragrant pure beauty would last forever.

It is one day fearing I am losing my mind to weakness, the next seeing the light of joy in life again at the end of the tunnel.

It is submitting to God my last shred of security and wondering how much harder I can cling.

It is realizing that life is too short to not take the time for the little things we don't have time for.

It is a continuous ache seeing couples and families with fathers interact.

It is one day not able to feel the sun's rays and the next able to rejoice in the beauty this life does hold.

It is pulling new gray hair every day that affirm I've aged in many ways.

It is admitting that I really do need people and that they are Christ's hands and feet.

It is the reality of my name alone on the new checks that came.

It is appreciating senseless gestures of kindness that mean so much.

It is remembering that God keeps His promises even while we wrestle with the "how."

It is realizing that what my house looks like doesn't matter; what my heart looks like does.

It is allowing myself to stay in my pajamas when greeting the day looks daunting.

It is knowing that despair can be all-consuming and understanding that lack of hope in tomorrow.

It is pruning a shrub, knowing I'm doing it all wrong.

It is being engulfed with memories, finding the marker in a book Vernon and I were reading together.

It is eyes blurring, browsing recipes that he loved.

It is having the chair he died in become my favorite.

It is a picnic at the graveyard, wondering at the untold stories beneath the stones.

It is needing coffee to get through my day and then waiting for the nights to end.

It is accepting that though the sun may not shine today, it will in some tomorrow.

It is praying that somehow God can use my sorrow.

Saturday, August 4, 2007

I recently spent some time rereading past posts and I was taken aback at the intensity of my despair in months past. I guess I hadn't realized how deep my grief was and how far I have actually come in healing. Praise God He is not inactive in what can even seem His silence. The growing pains I've experienced have resulted in a woman more confident in her Saviour. This path through mourning I walk is with His hand in mine. He has given me a new hope for tomorrow. I can feel the sun's rays again. I can smell the lilies bloom. I can see my children smile. And while I am not naïve to the fact that the years ahead will hold the taste of trials of their own, I now know, as only those can know who have danced with death, that God's grace overpowers all. His promises have been played out in my life and I owe my joy to Him alone. Frederick Buechner wrote, "Joy is a mystery because it can happen anywhere, anytime, even under the most unpromising circumstances, even in the midst of suffering, with tears in its eyes."

The children continue to grieve in their own time and ways. The girls were playing recently and I heard Kezia say she was bringing flowers to Daddy because he was dying. I wanted to shake her and say, "Why does he have to be dying?! Why can't life just be normal in your play reenactment?" But I realize that, sadly, for this little girl, what she remembers is a life where her Daddy is dying. This hurts to my very core.

Last night as Tia and I lay in bed together whispering make-believe stories, she weaved this tale that I find full of untold meaning. She told of a man who had a cat who was very dear to him. The cat died and the man took it to church weeping (her words) and placed it in the offering.

And a few nights back as we were singing Vernon's favorite song, "Lord, with Glowing Heart I Praise Thee", one of my sons burst into tears; the other one and I got through another stanza before we joined him in his grief. It seemed we could almost hear Vernon singing it.

Faith does not always come from quiet contemplation or meditation. It is sometimes born among the raging of questions with no answers, pain with no relief, hope that has no reason to exist. ~ Randy Becton

Tuesday, August 7, 2007

Nearly six months ago, we sang "Oh Come, Angel Band" and they came and took my husband home. I cannot describe the peace it gives to imagine him worshiping before the Throne. And though these months have been dark and the path hard and long, it is with gratefulness to my Father I can yet praise Him in song. Won't you join me in song with a hymn sing on my lawn this next Tuesday evening, August 14th (Vernon's birth date)? Bring your lawn chairs and a finger food to share if you like. We are limited on a dispersal time because of nightfall so we'll aim to start singing by 7:00 P.M. but you can come as early as 6:00 P.M. for fellowship and finger food.

Wednesday, August 15, 2007

Surely the presence of the Lord was in this place. The truths of the scriptures and sentiments expressed in those old, tried-and-true hymns of the faith were a balm to our souls as we sang to the glory of the Father. We sang of needing Him every hour. We beseeched His mercy for our sins, recognizing Him as our God, our Help in ages past. Acknowledging in our limited understanding His moving in mysterious ways in our lives, yet able to praise Him with a glowing heart. We told our burdens to Jesus, asking our Savior to lead us all the way. We bade our soul be still over life's tempestuous sea. We sang of the greatness of His faithfulness and could with luster choir it was well with our souls. May Jesus Christ be praised!

As we gathered in gratefulness of Vernon's life here on earth, it seemed fitting to think he was singing with us, though his song now made perfect in glory, already having finished his race. We, of course, yet wait that joy set before us. Yet the presence of the dear friends and family who assembled themselves last evening on my lawn represent my joy here below; those who have continuously encouraged, interceded and cried with me on this journey. I thank you.

Sunday, August 19, 2007

A song that spoke to me in church today from the Presbyterian Psalter:

Amid the battle shock
My song shall still resound;
Then joyful offerings I will bring,
Jehovah's praise my heart shall sing.

Sunday, August 26, 2007

It was one year ago we assembled here in our living room with many friends and loved ones while Vernon was anointed with oil according to James 5:13. Our prayer then was that God would gain as much glory and gratitude if He chose not to heal Vernon as He surely would if He did heal him from the cancer. It is with tears I now sit here alone, pondering the glory that might have been wrought our merciful Father by His choice.

A husband fills many roles: friend, lover, father to my children, spiritual leader, provider, repairman… the list goes on. But what I find myself mourning and yearning for is the friendship we shared. How I miss the man who cared about my hurts, my joys and the little things in life. The one who knew me in and out, who loved my ups, bore with my downs. Who knew what I was going to say sometimes before I could say it. Who shared my views or at least humored me in them. Who was there, day in, day out. Oh, the ache of loneliness for a friendship gone. I may have a hundred friends, many of them very dear, but none can begin to compare to the friend that I knew in my husband. It is a lonely road to be half of what was once one.

Many people ask about school. I am grateful my children will not need to face a change in their schooling this coming year. Thanks to the generosity of givers who knew Vernon's passion for their education, my oldest three children are again enrolled at Veritas Academy. My oldest is entering 7th grade, which feels like a challenging phase, and Vernon's missing active and interested involvement in their academic studies looms large before me. I will teach my youngest Kindergarten at home.

I sat with tears streaming one day, asking myself, "Why am I crying?" The conclusion I reached was that though my life is at times seemingly unbearably sad, yet I have a God who is incomprehensibly good. And though these statements would appear contradictory, grace assures us they are not. Perhaps one needs to be in the position of where God has stripped you of your dearest earthly possession, and yet He has blessed you in amazing abundance, before beginning to be able to grasp this difficult aspect of grace. That unexplainable, undeserved favor even in what would appear deplorable conditions - not despite of - even more so in the valley. So though my tears flow, I know I bask in a grace I'll never fully realize till I bow before His throne. But for now, it is enough to daily partake of this mystery: its source, sufficiency, strength, and sweetness.

Nothing before,
nothing behind;
the steps of faith
fall on the seeming
void and find
the rock beneath.

~ John Greenleaf Whittier, 1807-1892

Friday, August 31, 2007

Perhaps it is the predominantly traditional family county I live in, perhaps it is yet finding my footing on this awkward terrain, but I find it difficult to get used to this single-parent business. My boys have developed a passion for fishing which has necessitated a trip to Cabela's and multiple journeys to the local sportsman shop. I can't walk into those places with my tribe in tow without feeling like every eye is upon me. And the questions and comments one must endure.

Countless times I hear the question, "Are they all yours?!" There are only four of them! Do I look that overwhelmed? And when the innocent offender says: "My, you must have your hands full!" I want to shout at them, "You have no idea!" But I have learned to smile sweetly, agree politely and make my exit. They don't have the time, I don't have the time, and no doubt they have a story of their own. Or when I get the question regarding the children, "Will there be more?" (once again by the innocent clerk or waitress) I resist my urge to blast them by sarcastically shouting that there is no dad, so of course not! But instead I feebly reply, "I don't think so." It is much easier to withhold truth than to endure its ensuing awkwardness. Plus, I can't quite come up with a casual way of saying, "'Um, well, actually my husband died of cancer."

God give us all gracious words for those we meet each day.

Saturday, September 1, 2007

> Twelve years ago today,
> Vernon held his firstborn tenderly with tears.
> The awe and responsibility of that new life
> is what began my husband's sobering and serious
> journey deeper into his faith.
> How that fatherly absence is sorely felt
> as my son now reaches
> this milestone of his own,
> merging from boyhood to man.

Oh Thou whose mercy guides my way,
Though now it seems severe,
Forbid my unbelief to say
There is no mercy here!

~ Unknown Author

Sunday, September 2, 2007

The pastor spoke of God's love and of His working all things out for our good, of trials being blessings. I had to walk out early, my eyes blurred with tears. I know these truths; I live them every day. Yet today, they were salt on a wound, licked fresh from recent lacerations: birthdays, news of a tragic death, a dream about my beloved, sensing my husband's absence like a raw throb this morning, feelings of complete inadequacy in child rearing, floundering in the bottom of a sinner's pit, the fall bite in the air bringing difficult memories and a chill that can't be warmed. "God of my weary years, God of my silent tears," might I feel Your love this day. I wonder if You could, in Your mercy, give me just a glimpse of that good You are working out through my affliction.

In my ensuing melancholy this afternoon, I picked up J. C. Ryle's book *Holiness* off the bookshelf, hungry for something my husband had absorbed. I read: "When we cannot see the reason of God's dealings, our duty is to hold our peace and believe." And then this which Vernon had heavily highlighted: "If there is no cross, there will be no crown."

By His grace alone, I shall hold my peace while struggling under this cross.

Monday, September 3, 2007

Thirty-eight years ago today, in a small town in Michigan, a young unwed mother gave birth (abortion not yet legal). Days later, that baby girl graced the home of a Christian family with three young boys of their own. I will be forever grateful for that working of my Sovereign Lord. The bond formed between my mother and I was stronger than blood and I will always be grateful for my father's sacrifice and his example in eternal matters. And although my brothers teased me mercilessly through childhood, they also protected and respected me and remain a valued part of my life today. Then, when I married Vernon, I joined a family who has become to me as dear as my own. Although I grew up without sisters, I now have a total of eleven sisters-in-law and count each one as a friend. Family, despite the accompanying challenges and heartaches, is one of those mercies our Father in Heaven grants us. How blessed I am with these ties that bind.

Christians are like the flowers in a garden, that have each of them the dew of Heaven, which, being shaken with the wind, they let fall at each other's roots, whereby they are jointly nourished, and become nourishers of each other.
~ John Bunyan, 1628-1688

Thursday, September 13, 2007

It is with some sighs of relief we now have several weeks of school behind us. It is extremely difficult to face this part of life without Vernon, school bringing with it so many memories of his involvement. Seems like we are yet establishing this "new normal" of our lives; the end of school last year being in merely survival mode. The child who was going to run away and hide in the cornfield the first day of school is still living with us and now prays that the school year will go fast. And I vacillate between being encouraged by the maturity and renewed respect I see in my adolescent, to reeling under his frustrated expressions both brought about by the strict structure and workload our school demands.

I admit I was ready by summer vacation's end to turn, especially my boys, over to someone else's authority and have come to doubt the wisdom of a single mom homeschooling. I believe they need the firm authority structure of someone besides a weak mother. And as I now seem to fit into that undesirable category called a "single mom", I realize that in many ways it really does "take a village." And I am most grateful for the community of support I receive from God's people.

When I count my blessings, naming them one by one, I am astounded by what God has done. I am also convicted in my whining about wondering what good has come by the trials from which we've come. I feel like the Israelites who moaned over their past leeks and onions, not recognizing the "lifetime warrantee" of the sandals on their feet. And the glimpses of the good that have indeed come by Vernon's life and death through the testimonies of those impacted nourish my wound as a healing salve. My children continue to struggle and manifestations of their grief are unique to each one.

As if my own heartache isn't enough of a throb, reminders of my husband's absence are frequent. I received a call today from a lady who hadn't known about Vernon's death requesting his landscaping services. Cancer treatment bills addressed to him continue to arrive on a regular basis.

But I sense a progress in my healing as well. I no longer feel the jab of sharp pain when I pass a white work truck. And I think I am getting used to coming home to a dark house without him. And baking for others helps ease the loss of my husband's appreciation.

I've been spending considerable time lately deciding on a gravestone for Vernon. This final memorial representing his life and death in stone is important to me. And in attempting to involve my children in the process, I am needing to be patient and creative in appeasing everyone involved. My children seem to be quite comfortable in cemeteries by now. I need to remind my girls that not all people would appreciate them crawling on their loved ones' gravestones. The cemetery where Vernon's earthly shell lies is now peacefully surrounded by tall cornfields and is a quiet respite from the rush of life.

A virtual stranger recently came up to me with these words: "They say joy comes in the morning - did your morning come yet?" In my ensuing shock I believe I answered with a resounding "no". It had already been a difficult day.

There are two ways of getting out of a trial. One is to simply try to get rid of the trial, and be thankful when it is over. The other is to recognize the trial as a challenge from God to claim a larger blessing than we have ever had, and to hail it with delight as an opportunity of obtaining a larger measure of Divine grace... ~ A. B. Simpson

Sunday, September 16, 2007

In reflecting on those women I know whose loved one is diagnosed with a terminal illness, and in being reminded of my own journey when I see this played out...

I'd like to write a tribute to the woman
who daily watches her dreams die;
to the one who stands beside her husband
knowing there comes that final goodbye.
Watching the man she loves

wither before her eyes;
aching as he fades from being her protector
and the one able to provide.
As she learns the steps to this delicate dance
of changing roles;
the weight she carries a heavy load
and hers to carry alone.
God, give her strength to stand.

Wednesday, September 19, 2007

I observe my children in their particular modes of learning to live and love life without Daddy. And my heart aches as I absorb their hurts with them. How we all long for him and wonder if we will ever again feel whole. I see my firstborn carry his grief; it is like watching a lad carry a man's load. And the son much like his father wears his daddy's old t-shirts and has claimed his dad's Bible for his own. The girl Daddy called "princess", with her tender heart and tears, cries easily yet picks herself up from her grief and goes on with her fairy tale way. And the youngest one admitted the other day she doesn't understand how Daddy's body can lie in the ground yet he be in this place called heaven.

We live life as if it were a motion picture. Loss turns life into a snapshot. The movement stops; everything freezes. We find ourselves looking at picture albums to remember the motion pictures of our lives that once was but can no longer be. ~ Jerry Sittser

We are not necessarily doubting that God will do the best for us; we are wondering how painful the best will turn out to be. ~ C.S. Lewis

Tuesday, September 25, 2007

Just when I think I have conquered an area in this grief's battle, it comes back full-force. I need to pray for emotional stability, especially Lord's Day mornings as they can be challenging days.

Vernon and I used to often walk around together in our gardens in the evening. Recently as I once again strolled alone, I recognized some slow and silent healing as I seem, somehow, better accustomed to the harsh loneliness.

In other ways, I feel like I am coming out of a distant fog. I have difficulty remembering much of what occurred during and after the trauma of losing Vernon. And I am finding stamina to tackle some projects that evoke painful memories.

A friend has offered to put together photo memory albums for each of my children of them and their Daddy, so I have been spending hours going through the past years in print. The range of emotions experienced run the gamut. My heart swells with pride and love at the man I see playing with them, being the daddy we took for granted. And the progression of sadness I see in my children's countenances over the time he was sick startles me now. When I compare the innocent joy and ease of living in the snapshots of life before diagnosis, I am soberly reminded how quickly life can change.

A friend commented recently how I pour so much of myself into my children. After reflecting on her words, I realize that my fierce love for them comes in part that they are what I have of Vernon; all I will ever have to tangibly show of him and of our love together. Countless are the times I tell my brown-eyed girl how glad I am that she has her Daddy's eyes. Or I am reminded of Vernon in my sons with temperaments much like their father's. As much as I am frustrated with and feel hopelessly inadequate in rearing them, I daily thank God for the treasures they are.

I am alarmed, at times, with my disjointed view of God. Sometimes I think, "Surely He would not allow another tragedy to come upon me." And then, being the frail "out of Adam's rib" creation that I am, I worry. I worry about my health, my children being raised in the manner they should be, about the future: finances, housing, school; the list is endless. I daily need to ask my Heavenly Husband's forgiveness for not resting in His plan, whatever that may be. And He, gently and consistently, to my gratitude and shame, reminds me that He will provide for my every need.

Choose for us, God, not let our weak preferring
Cheat us of good Thou hast for us designed.
Choose for us God - Thy wisdom is unerring,
And we are fools and blind.

~ W.H. Burleigh, 1812 - 1871

Monday, October 1, 2007

Last week my five-year old said to me: "Mommy, I know a 'trick.'" She continued, "Daddy didn't really die." Oh, wee, darling girl, would that it were true. I, too, sometimes wonder if it can be real. But then, how many lonely days and dreadful nights can pass without the reality of the loved one lost not be painfully, permanently embedded? No, this is no trick, no bad dream from which we might yet awaken. No amount of denial could deny our present life of loss. It does not include Daddy and we continue to reel under our pain. Tears come in unexpected moments. At times I think we'll be ok, at others I am sure we will never recover.

But just as when fall sunshine pours through freshly washed windows, so God gives us "strength for today and bright hope for tomorrow." Great His faithfulness will be if we but accept and believe. And I can echo with the Crusaders' Hymn "Beautiful Savior": "He makes our sorrowing spirit sing." And as the preacher spoke yesterday: "We make of grace too small a thing."

It is well to bear in mind when we wince beneath the rod that we cannot expect to heal the deep wound of bereavement with one small application of comfort. Sorrow is given for a more important purpose than to be thus easily erased. God's comfort, however, gives a new and blessed aspect to our trials, and, if diligently sought and applied will in time not only heal, but leave as well a cross-shaped scar of grace upon our enriched souls!
~ Henry G. Bosch

Wednesday, October 3, 2007

Tonight is the annual parade at the local fair, an event we haven't missed as a family since our firstborn was old enough to enjoy it. I actually bribed the children to not go tonight, so strongly was my aversion to going this year without Vernon.

> I will pass
> on this year's parade -
> the gaudy noises
> and the frivolity of the Fair
> assaulting my grief
> that would rather curl up in a tight cocoon
> than ride the merry go round of emotions -
> family memories of the past

painfully present.
It's a cotton candy stick
I'll leave untouched this year
not having to deal with that empty chair -
nor hear the bands
and be a clown with a painted on smile

Sunday, October 7, 2007

Today was Tovi's 10th birthday. This son, so like his father in physique, temper and passion for life. His brown eyes dancing, his yearning for spiritual perfection; much of his Daddy mirrored in him.

I continue to have this strong aversion to birthdays without Vernon, his absence seemingly unjustifiable.

And I find myself repeatedly arguing with God over why He would take my husband and leave me a widow with four fatherless children who, according to my human understanding, very much need a dad.

I am duly admonished by the following:

Whenever, therefore, you find yourself disposed to uneasiness or murmuring at anything that is the effect of God's providence over you, you must look upon yourself as denying either the wisdom or goodness of God.

~ Wm Law

Let us be very careful of thinking, on the one hand, that we have no work assigned us to do, or, on the other hand, that what we have assigned to us is not the right thing for us. If ever we can say in our hearts to God, in reference to any daily duty, 'This is not my place; I would choose something dearer; I am capable of something higher;' we are guilty not only of rebellion, but of blasphemy. It is equivalent to saying, not only, 'My heart revolts against Thy

commands,' but 'Thy commands are unwise; Thine Almighty guidance is unskillful; Thine omniscient eye has mistaken the capacities of Thy creature; Thine infinite love is indifferent to the welfare of Thy child.
~ Elizabeth Charles, 1828-1896

Saturday, October 20, 2007

God's grace continues to encourage:
A recent weekend together with my family, precious beyond defining.
My children spending countless hours playing on our newly paved driveway compliments of my father-in-law, in anticipation of making the winter trek up the steep incline to the road easier.
Caring people who remembered with floral deliveries the eight month anniversary date of Vernon's passing.
Warm, sunny fall days easing the drear of this season.
Obvious progress in healing both in myself and the children - though our tears haven't ceased, I sense a strength evolving.

He leads us through storm and sunshine; through the valley of sorrows and into the green pastures. What we have to do is to follow trustingly, always ready to acknowledge His goodness and mercy, without fear of what may come, - because we know that 'the Lord is our Shepherd.' ~ A.H.S.

Tuesday, October 30, 2007

I hear that some wonder in my cyber silence if I am doing okay or if they should be concerned. Bless you for caring; I feel cherished. I fear I tend to write on the site mostly when I am absorbed in my melancholy.
"The sun will come out tomorrow..." little Orphan Annie sang. The sun has come out again after multiple successive days

of rain and drear. And in many ways the sun shines once more in my soul. I hesitate to speak too prematurely, however, having come to know this roller coaster ride so well, but I must tell you I do feel rays previously blocked by clouds. I no longer dread all my tomorrows. I can now believe that I might possibly know true joy again. Yet I am facing the upcoming holiday season and already cringe at the thought of tinsel with my tears.

Don't get me wrong, I haven't moved to Easy Street. Just last night I sat weeping over my children, missing their Dad's direction more than I could ever say. I wonder at times if, in the weariness and distraction of my grief, I have caused irreparable damage to them by neglecting to train them as I should. I often wonder what Vernon would say or do in a situation. And honestly, I don't always like my answers.

One person I look forward to meeting in Heaven is Mrs. Chas. E. Cowman. She compiled the popular devotional book *Streams In The Desert*. She also compiled a book entitled simply *Consolation*. I love her simple forward consisting only of this: "I dedicate this volume to the largest household in the world, the household of the sorrowing."

And a friend with a definite limp to their gait shared that someone had once told them when talking about Jacob wrestling with the angel, "Never trust a person that doesn't walk with a limp." I agree that those who have wrestled with God and have not won realize a victory only those who are battle-worn can understand.

I request your prayers for wisdom in direction concerning some future issues. The time has come for some decisions to be pursued and they appear quite daunting.

Unanswered yet? Faith cannot be unanswered,
Her feet are firmly planted on the Rock...

She knows Omnipotence has heard her prayer,
And cries, 'It shall be done' - sometime, somewhere.'

~ Ophelia G. Browning

Sunday, November 4, 2007

When pressed with burdens and troubles too complicated to put into words and too mysterious to tell or understand, how sweet it is to fall back into His blessed arms, and just sob out the sorrow that we cannot speak!
~ Unknown Author

Life as I now live it...

Involves being so tired of fighting tears overcome with love and sorrow over the man that no longer is. It's finding my youngest child crying in her closet wanting to be in Heaven with her Daddy. It was alternately crying and laughing my way through C. S. Lewis' *A Grief Observed,* re-reading portions aloud to my eldest son who agreed with me on the accuracy of his portrayal of the grieving process.

It is being so lonely for my husband that I find even the instruction of my GPS a welcome adult voice and the sound of the washing machine on a weekend evening somehow comforting. It is being invited to a widow's supper and finding it oddly gratifying.

It is abhorring my lack of compassion over others' heartaches, so absorbed in my own. It is resenting this wound that never heals. It is begging God to let my affliction count for something. It is seeking to be content without the intimacy of the relationship He removed from me. It is needing to turn to Him for support, counsel and fulfillment.

It is wallowing in my sinfulness this day, wanting my husband so badly I cannot submit to my Sovereign God's divine will and way. It is wanting to give every one of my children away, feeling my utter ineptness in single parenting. It is looking at this upcoming season of thankfulness and joy with complete lack of gratitude and cheer.

Yet, it is repenting of my earthly fears. It is being blessed with a friend who came up to me at church this morning and hearing her gently say "I'm sensing this morning isn't the best of days." It is asking God to give a special blessing to the father of my son's friend who has been giving them the "therapy" of taking them to do what they most love to do these days: go fishing. It is accepting as a personal gift from God the unusually warm late fall days. It is being humbly reminded of the daily blessings I have with the continuing arrival of the boxes and cards I yet receive from those reminding me of their care. It is the sweetness of my daughter's frequent kisses expressing her love. It is being duly admonished by one who knows well the deep waters of the power in God's Word.

In fleeing for refuge beneath the shadow of God's wing, we will always find more in God than we had seen or known before.
~ William Taylor

Wednesday, November 7, 2007

"God help!" is often the feeble prayer that leaves my lips. I know not how to formulate my needs to the One who knows them anyway.

It is a curious blend, this: trying to hang on to the old yet grasp for the new. In my emotional disability wrought about by grief, I struggle for discernment in what could be decisions regretted later.

I dig out the fall bulbs with spadefuls of nostalgia. Though we couldn't dig together last year, at least he was still with me; the fall perennial cleanup always a favorite task of his. Each day I pass by a business where Vernon used to pour his devotion into their landscaping maintenance. I sometimes now wince as I view their faltering attempts.

Unless you've dusted the picture frames of your loved one when that is all you have, I don't suppose I can convey the emotions encompassed in that act. I study his face, his features, longing for him in flesh again. Photographic memories no match for the reality of yesterday.

We sang an unfamiliar hymn in church on Sunday and I was touched by the words in remembering Vernon. I was not alone. Last night one of my children brought the hymnals and requested we learn this one as a family; he, too, having thoughts of his Daddy gone on before, his battle won, ours still to own.

For All the Saints
Who from their labors rest,
Who Thee by faith before the world confessed,
Thy Name, O Jesus, be forever blest.

Thou wast their Rock, their Fortress and their Might;
Thou, Lord, their Captain in the well-fought fight.
Thou, in the darkness drear, their one true Light

O May Thy soldiers, faithful, true and bold,
Fight as the saints who nobly fought of old,
And win with them the victor's crown of gold.

O blest communion, fellowship divine!
We feebly struggle, they in glory shine;
Yet all are one in Thee, for all are Thine:

And when the fight is fierce, the warfare long,
Steals on the ear the distant triumph song,
And hearts are brave again, and arms are strong:

From earth's wide bounds, from ocean's farthest coast,
Through gates of pearl streams in the countless host,
Singing to Father, Son, and Holy Ghost:

Alleluia, Alleluia!

~ "For All The Saints" by William How, 1864

Thursday, November 8, 2007

Mere months after Vernon's death, his sister Liz, just one year older than he, was diagnosed with lymphoma. She has been on a steady chemo and Vitamin C regimen since July. Many of you ask about her as I had requested prayer for the family that reeled under this news so soon after Vernon's battle. Today she writes:

I hardly know how to express the gratitude we feel since we received the good news that my blood is clear of cancer cells. I know God doesn't answer everyone's prayer for healing as He did mine, and I feel unworthy of healing - but I know God is sovereign, He makes no mistakes, His ways are not my ways, His thoughts are higher than mine. God's grace is sufficient for our and your needs. God bless each one for interceding on my behalf. I want to continue to live my life each day as though it were my last, looking for opportunities to touch other people's lives. ~ Liz Hershberger

"Joy and pain can live in the same house. Neither should deny the other."
~ Tan Neng

(Author's note: Liz finished her earthly journey January 25, 2011.)

Friday, November 16, 2007

As if my own waves of grief are not unpredictable enough to deal with, I glanced over last night to see my eldest daughter folding laundry with tears streaming down her face. Missing her Daddy was the reason when I asked her source of woe. We sat holding each other amidst socks and towels, weeping and reminiscing. My youngest, not willing herself to join in, tried to make light of the situation by handing us wash clothes to use for tissues and then beginning with "knock knock" jokes. Ah, this is the business of grief work. As much as we'd like to think it is each one in their own time in their own way, it seems more like that laundry: just when you think you've caught up, there is another load.

It might be nice to have the liberty of a bear's hibernation this fall and winter. First there is Thanksgiving and Christmas to get through, then it will be our anniversary in January, followed by the anniversary of his death in February. I long already for the crocus with its first sign of spring.

I have started the lighting of many candles. These fall evenings where darkness falls early too easily mirrors my mood of the season. The flicker of the flame somehow giving hope in a tranquility to come.

Our sheets were flannel because he loved flannel. They were blue with brown leaves because he loved fall foliage. I took them to the thrift store. Memories need no longer torment each night, longing for him, longing for the love we shared.

I verbalized to a friend how I longed for this intense pain to mutate in healing to rather a deep sadness. She, who had never known any great loss and unable to comprehend the depth of this pain, commented that she would never want to reduce her love and commitment to her husband to a mere sad memory. It was Shakespeare who said: "Everyone can master a grief but he that has it."

Six years ago tomorrow, I received the call from my father that my mother had reached her Heavenly home. They were an ocean away, seeking yet another desperate treatment for the cancer that ravaged her body. It was the culmination of an eight-year battle with that beast that eats away at health and hearts and homes. It was this fight with life and death, with health and healing, that led to the age-old struggle between my God and I over His complete sovereignty. My mother believed God would heal her. She believed her faith was weak. I knew as I watched her body shrivel and her soul suffer that there was no comfort in this sort of God, who makes so much depend on weak creatures. The battle that I fought to understand His sovereignty would prove to be of significant value when my own husband's cancer took his life in only seven months. And it is my firm belief in this omniscient God that encourages me to keep clinging to His love and mercy.

Truly this is a grief, and I must bear it. ~ Jeremiah 10:19 KJV

Thursday, November 22, 2007

On this day of thanksgiving, I desire to bring glory to the Giver of all good gifts, though we as finite creatures may not recognize them as such. I am grateful for the saints who helped field the array of arrows from the evil one who tried to hinder me from bringing my sacrifice of praise this day, whether those whose lives closely intersect with mine or those faithful in prayer across the miles.

This past week was wrought with hurt and heartache and I doubt I have cried this many tears since the months immediately following Vernon's death. Yet I remain grateful for God's love and grace that is beyond my comprehension and most certainly my deservation. I am grateful for the tangible expressions of His love through His people. I am grateful for how He more and more opens my eyes to His hidden mercies. I am grateful for my dear children who are what I have of the one I mourn and who are of immeasurable value in my giving of thanks.

Many ask how I will spend this day. Many offered to share their homes and their tables. But it seems fitting for my children and I to break bread and share thanks with the other mourners who loved Vernon deeply: his dear parents.

Amidst my list of blessings infinite
Stands this the foremost, that my heart has bled;
For all I bless Thee, most for the severe.

~ Hugh Macmillan

Saturday, December 1, 2007

With my matter-of-fact mourning, I had resigned myself to the holidays but I failed to factor in my children's feelings. These are trying times. This year as we sing carols by candle light, it is not the same with one missing from our choir. And unless you have held your child, her body racked with uncontrollable sobs night after night, missing her Daddy now in heaven, I cannot express to you that heart-wrenching pain. Another talks of Daddy with sort of a pained puzzlement at his absence. One tries to hide the pain but bursts of anger sometimes give way. And I have no words to convey the helpless feeling that comes from listening to yet another child cry himself to sleep because he hasn't a father. Yet amid our torrents of tears, we worship the Star of Bethlehem. And Vernon's mom remarked how she is comforted by thinking of Vernon spending his first Christmas singing in the heavenly choir.

Be near me, Lord Jesus,
I ask Thee to stay...
Bless all the dear children
In Thy tender care
And fit us for heaven
To live with Thee there.

~ Charles H. Gabriel, 1892

Saturday, December 8, 2007

Jesus always loved to comfort. He loves to put little candles in the darkened chambers of sorrow. ~ J.R. Miller

He does indeed bring glimpses of His light and warmth into our lives these cold December days. He hath not left me comfortless, just as He promised in John 14:18.

On my son's dresser sits a framed snapshot of him and his daddy flying a kite together. Perhaps that is why now the lad can often be found outside running against the wind. Every time I see him out alone with streamers trailing, it is hard to keep my tears from following. I wonder if in some sense he feels close to his father or attempts to recapture the carefree joy of those days.

My kindergartener, who cannot yet read, enjoys innocently copying letters off of anything she sees so I often find interesting scraps of paper lying around with her laboriously determined script. Today I picked up one that caused me to wince. It read: "Praxair Health Care, For all your home infusion needs, call: 1-800..."

The fact that tears and tissues are such a part of our life was made apparent recently as the children were crafting tiny Christmas ornaments. Among the collection of wreaths and snowman and santa hats, they had made a tiny tissue box. No doubt it will be a befitting reminder when we find it in our ornament collection in the years to come.

Some of you have no doubt observed I have trouble at times referring to my husband in past tense. Thank you for pretending not to notice as I stumble over the words. And it is truly acceptable for you to talk about your husband and your marriage. And when you see tears in my eyes, I do not mind if you disregard them, nor do I mind if you hand me a tissue. It is ok if you cry with me and it is just as alright if you don't. Mourners do not ask for your tears, only your understanding.

I recently spent sweet hours going through some files Vernon kept of all our correspondence while we were dating, a honeymoon journal, and anniversary cards. I read every note and love letter and was awed by what a wonderful man he was and how very much I loved him. It was refreshing to reminisce of our young love before the years of marriage that brought along babies and toddlers and all the stuff of life, and then of course that most painful stress of the time from diagnosis till death.

Our hearts are heavy lately as Vernon's mother's macular degenerative disease seems to be progressing at a more rapid rate. She is healthy and active and loves to read and this is hard to bear. We had a beautiful anointing service the other evening and the Spirit's presence was felt. Brought back reminders, however, of another anointing service in which God was pleased to not bring about the only healing that our earthly-minded hearts can understand.

Small were my faith should it weakly falter,
Now that the roses have ceased to grow;
Frail were the trust that now should alter,
Doubting His love when the storm clouds blow.
If I trust Him once,
I must trust Him ever...

~ Song of a Bird in a Winter Storm

Thursday, December 13, 2007

Countless tales of heartache related to me in the past weeks cause me to ponder all these things in my heart while phrases of Christmas carols run alternately through my head.

O Come, all ye faithful, though ye feel not *joyful and triumphant.* So many heartaches, so much pain, different stories, different names. Each one's sorrow unique in chapters and pages alone. To the tired, to the sad, *Good Christian Men Rejoice.* Check our smiles at the door, end our masquerade. Let's own our hurt but claim our hope. *Jesus Christ was born for this.*

Senseless shootings, *peace on earth. God and sinners reconciled.* Brain tumor growing in my friend's head, a young mother with children yet to raise - *Joy to the World?* Leukemia diagnosed in a boy only entering the prime of his youth, *O repeat the sounding joy. Our sins and sorrows do yet grow* and we wait our *King to come.*

A mother with severely limited funds with which to feed her family. *Yea, Lord we greet Thee, this happy morning.* A spouse has left to remarry another. Or the wife of the alcoholic gambler, *far as the curse is found*. A mourner who counts the days till Christmas is over, *death's dark shadows put to flight*. And so many more who confess they can not see the tinsel shine, *Light and life to all He brings*.

O Come, O Come, Emmanuel, disperse the gloomy clouds of night though our midnights are often not clear and sleep eludes us *beneath life's crushing load*. May we, through our tear-blurred vision, lift our voices and sing: *Glory to God, all glory in the highest*.

Sunday, December 30, 2007

"My only comfort in life and in death is that I am not my own, but belong - body and soul, to my faithful Savior Jesus Christ." Out of the Heidelberg Catechism (first published in 1563), this was one of Vernon's favorite affirmations of his faith and was to become even more apt as his earthly life faded.

On a hilltop in Elverson sits a newly erected gravestone marking the life and body of the one I mourn. The absence of my best friend and my children's father are a daily void with depths unfathomed.

Yet I believe it is to suggest that my Sovereign Father knows not what is best, when I, in my loss, take my eyes off believing that I can trust Him for what He hath done in taking the life of one so young and needed. Rather, I must repeatedly put my hand over my mouth, like Job, and as Christ taught us to pray: "Thy will be done, on earth, as it is in Heaven." (Matthew 6:10 KJV)

This week would be our fourteenth wedding anniversary. Sometimes after I talk with those who celebrated more than fifty years as one, I wonder, what do I know of love and loss? But then I see my fatherless little ones and face the many years ahead alone and I realize submission to my loss as part of my cross.

There is a peace that cometh after sorrow,
Of hope surrendered, not of hope fulfilled;
A peace that looketh not upon tomorrow,
But calmly on a tempest that it stilled.

A peace that lives not now in joy's excesses,
Nor in the happy life of love secure;
But in the unerring strength the heart possesses,
Of conflicts won while learning to endure.

~ Streams in the Desert

Tuesday, January 8, 2008

When will I learn, I wonder, that God's work in me is never through? When will I realize that He never ceases to require of me to call on the One who is worthy of bringing glory to? He has proved His love time and time again; how can I demand more than what He chooses to give? May my Saviour rescue me from my pit of despair, may I release to Him this burden I bear. I need my Prince of Peace to reclaim my soul, alight on me, make me whole. In my sin and in my shame, I disgrace His name, I writhe in discontent, I wrestle with my pain. Then, in a classic case of grace, He holds out His hand, I reach up with mine, and in Him once more His strength I find.

Remember your word to your servant, in which you have made me hope. This is my comfort in my affliction, that your promise gives me life.
~ Psalm 119:49-50 ESV

Sunday, January 13, 2008

We come
to partake of the blood
and body of Christ

We come
some outwardly broken
others with hidden fractures

We are
humbled
desperate for this
means of grace

We leave
still broken
yet strengthened
by His promise

We are His
bought with the
ultimate price
His life and sacrifice

We go again
into this world
holding this
Hope that we have

Wednesday, January 23, 2008

For this slight momentary affliction is preparing for us an eternal weight of glory beyond all comparison. ~ 2 Corinthians 4:17 ESV

This sanctifying process seems relentless: I have seen some rough weeks pass. . .

. . . my friend with the brain tumor thought to be benign. . . pathology report came back showing aggressive cancer.

. . . my children, no doubt in their grief's haze of confusion and anger, have been exhibiting behavior that leaves me alternately stunned and disturbed.

. . . repeated struggles with the sin of anxiety about the future as I am faced with decisions about work and school.

. . . facing memories of last year at this time, coupled with intense loneliness and awareness of my children's dire need of a dad.

. . . sometimes writhing in discontent and finding that I cannot say with the Apostle Paul, "I have learned, in whatever state I am, to be content."

Yet. . . for the present, I trust in that eternal end.

Sunday, January 27, 2008

I realized a facet of contentment this morning as I looked out my window and an unbidden prayer of thankfulness to God for this day left my lips. Any griever knows those thoughts don't come naturally. And anyone who knows me well, knows my extreme distaste for this season and of course that is presently compounded by memories of last year. So, I was startled by the actual gratitude I felt and could thank God for His gift.

And while on a walk yesterday I discovered a bright yellow dandelion blossom among the frozen landscape. How could this flower bloom in this bitter cold? To me, it was a replica of God's grace in my life.

Months ago, I had honored my youngest daughter request for a locket to wear around her neck with a photo of Daddy in it. I realized some healing has surely come to our hearts as the girls and I shared some laughter together the other day when her older sister attempted to grab Daddy out of the locket because she "wanted him." Later though, my five-year old admitted she doesn't remember Daddy holding her though she now carries him. There was no more laughter.

My boys are being blessed much lately. Men have been taking them to hockey games, to battle reenactments, to fishing expos, and along snowboarding. Yesterday they were given a basketball hoop. Elders, deacons, and friends have been reaching out to them with helpful instruction in areas like respect and attitude that Mom doesn't seem to have as much clout in. I am so grateful for the many who follow God's prescription for true religion in James 1:27 by caring for the widow and the fatherless.

I've been connecting lately with some fellow widows and widowers whose loss has been longer, and I am greatly encouraged by the assurance they give me of joy and hope for what will yet come. I used to not believe those words when I was told them soon after Vernon's death. It is easier now to be a believer in that hope after seeing much of what God has done.

I stood a mendicant of God before His royal throne and begged Him for one priceless gift that I could call my own. I took the gift from out His hand, but as I would depart I cried 'but Lord, this is a thorn… and it has pierced my heart. This is a strange, a hurtful gift which Thou hast given me.' He said 'My child I give good gifts and gave my best to thee.' I took it home, and though at first the cruel thorn hurt sore, As long years passed I learned at last to love it more and more. I learned He never gives a thorn without this added grace; He takes the thorn to pin aside the veil that hides His face.

~ The Thorn by Martha Snell Nicholson

Tuesday, February 12, 2008

For everything there is a season, and a time for every matter under heaven... ~ Ecclesiastes 3:1 ESV

So many of you have been graciously remembering the anniversary date of my husbands death. I have felt your prayers. However, as it now approaches one year ago that Vernon went to his heavenly home, my intent is that this will be my final Caring Bridge journal entry. I thank you for the interest and prayers you have expended on our behalf.

So many of you encouraged me with your kind and gracious words via guest book entries and personal e-mails. I assure you I am an unworthy vessel through which God's grace may have flowed; those who know me best know this to be true. I will miss the outlet this online journal has afforded. I will feel the inevitable loss of frequent contact with so many of you. I have made new friends, deepened bonds with older ones, and overall been greatly edified through the universal body of Christ. To all who came, who cared, who cried, and who prayed, I will forever remain grateful. Carie O'Leary said, "You may forget with whom you laughed, but you will never forget with whom you wept." Indeed, I knew not the loneliness of unshared sorrow. Yet, the needs of this world are many and we are each one called to go and do likewise in sharing the love of Christ.

And in no way do I imply my time of mourning is over. Mourning, in a sense, will never be over as we live on this sin-accursed earth. Complete healing will never be ours until we commune face-to-face with our Father in Heaven. Yet as earthly progress is afforded, a measured healing has come to this broken heart. Tears no longer come more easily than smiles. Life no longer feels like a sigh. The sharp stabbing pain that once consumed has graduated to a dull ache. The wound that at times felt mortal formed a scab and now we bear the scar. Another widow once told me, "The scar will last your whole life, but scars don't hurt." Yet, my daughter who required stitches on her forehead soon after her Daddy died remarked recently, "Mom, when I touch my scar, it still hurts." I would have to say the same goes for ours.

I tend to stage events either as life B.C. (before cancer) or life A.D. (after death). And then there is that haze of time consisting of about one year that defies a defining category; I still have trouble with memory of events that occurred between diagnosis and the months immediately following his death.

Yet life moves on. And though healing was both longed for and necessary, at times now, I find myself resenting it. Our mentioning of Daddy, while less painful, has also become less frequent. It seems peculiarly saddening to be moving beyond the year of the "first." Our lives are truly as a vapor. It does no good to hold our breath.

Many ask if I intend to stay here, since Pennsylvania is not my birthplace. But since my family is scattered and my mother gone to her heavenly home, Michigan does not call me. And since this is the home my children know, for now we will remain content living where we are. God alone knows what the future holds. My five-year old suggested recently that perhaps we could buy a house with a dad in it.

My God truly has supplied all my needs (Philippians 4:19) and the fact that I fail to keep His command about not worrying about the morrow is my own vice. Many a time I weep over the richness of His goodness to me and puzzle over what He is trying to tell me and why He bothers with me. I strive to be a wise steward of His blessings. So much of what lies ahead looms vast and frighteningly unknown. I simply must rest in God's promises and past provisions.

So, I thank you once more for having walked together with me on this path. One humbling lesson I learned was that I need people - God's people through whom He lives and moves and has His being. More importantly I learned His grace is merciful, plentiful, and senseless to my limited understanding. I live in awe of this God we serve. I eagerly await the day I can worship before His throne alongside my beloved. "May the circle be unbroken."

"Lie still, be strong, today!'

'But Lord, tomorrow -
what of tomorrow, Lord!
Shall there be rest from toil,
be joy for sorrow?'

'Did I not die for thee?
Do I not live for thee?
Leave me tomorrow.'"

~ Christina G. Rossetti

Acknowledgments

There are four people to whom I will remain forever indebted to. Many emails were exchanged day and night. These dear people received all the "behind the scenes" laments and concerns. Their medical knowledge coupled with their spiritual counsel kept me sane and stable. Fagel, Marge, Don and Marilee, I will *never* forget nor cease to be grateful for your friendship.

I must recognize Covenant Reformed Church of New Holland (now Zeltenreich Reformed Church). The fellowship and instruction my husband and I received worshipping together with the body there was the highlight of our weeks. My utmost respect and gratitude remain with Elder Clark Bearinger and Deacon Tim Bender who went well beyond their duties in ensuring that our every need was addressed. Thank you Tim and Wilma for the countless hours you invested.

I remain overwhelmed with the body of Christ represented locally and throughout the States through prayers and financial support. To the countless and nameless individuals who blessed us by caring, I thank you. So many instances of kindness and generosity went unrecorded, I would run the risk of excluding blessings, both large and small, if I attempted to list them. I could never mention all the people God used to bring glory to His name on this journey.

I gained a new appreciation for family - both mine and Vernon's - for their sustaining care. My tender love remains for Vernon's parents, Ben and Emma. The dignity with which they faced their loss can only result from their quiet confidence in a Sovereign Lord.

I am grateful for the immense help of my volunteer editors. Jenny Florio, your vision and encouragement played a huge role in this finished project. Andrea Kulp, you faced the daunting task of the first edit. Ervina Yoder, mere weeks after completing the final edit, the dreaded clouds came and you laid your firstborn in the ground.

And for Shawn Smucker in your professional aid in bringing all to completion.

About the Author

Sharon Stoltzfus lives in Bird-In-Hand, Pennsylvania with her husband Ammon and their combined six children. She continues trusting God for His grace as their children find their own way to the cross.

She is a member at Westminster Presbyterian Church.

She can be reached at sharonstoltzfus@gmail.com

Bibliography

1. George Herbert, "The Bag," 1633.

2. John Piper and David Powlison, *Don't Waste Your Cancer* (Wheaton, IL: Crossway 2006).

3. Octavius Winslow, "The Tried Believer Comforted" (www.gracegems.org).

4. Matthew Henry, *Matthew Henry's Commentary on the Whole Bible: Complete and Unabridged in Six Volumes* (Peabody, MA: Hendrickson Publishers 1991), 295.

5. John Greenleaf Whittier, "The Eternal Goodness."

6. F.B. Meyer, *My Daily Prayer.*

7. Suggs, Mary M, *All I Need: Meditations on the Master* (Grand Rapids, Mich: F.H. Revell 2001), October 26.

8. Brother Lawrence, *The Practice of the Presence of God,* Fifteenth Letter.

9. Joseph Hart, "How Good is the God We Adore."

10. Thomas Brooks, "The Funeral" (www.gracegems.org).

11. Carolyn Lunn, *Joy… Anyway!* (Kansas City: Beacon Hill Press of Kansas City 1992), 13-14, quoted in Carolyn Lunn, *Journaling Your Decembered Grief* (Kansas City: Beacon Hill Press of Kansas City 2001), 70.

12. C.S. Lewis, "Love's As Warm As Tears."

13. C.H. Spurgeon, *Morning and Evening,* January 16.

14. Daniel Russell, *Meditations for Men* (Nashville, TN: Abingdon Press 1945), 54.

15. C.S. Lewis, "Learning In War Time."

16. Daniel Russell, *Meditations for Men* (Nashville, TN: Abingdon Press 1945), 37.

17. John MacDuff, "Prayer at the Bedside of a Dying Believer" (www.gracegems.org).

18. John MacDuff, "Prayer for a Time of Bereavement" (www.gracegems.org).

19. Calvin Miller, *The Divine Symphony* (Minneapolis: Bethany 2000), 139.

20. Amy Carmichael, *Mountain Breezes*, "Will Not the End of Explain?"

21. Octavius Winslow, "The Godly Widow Confiding in the Widow's God" (www.gracegems.org).

22. J.R. Miller, "When the Song Begins!" (www.gracegems.org).

23. Thornton Burgess, *The Adventures of Bobby Raccoon*, p. 5.

24. Mrs. Chas. E. Cowman, *Consolation* (Los Angeles: Cowman Publications, Inc. 1950), 70.

25. C.S. Lewis, *The Silver Chair* (New York, NY: HarperCollins Publications 1981), 556.

26. Mary Baldwin, quoted in Mrs. Chas. E. Cowman, *Consolation* (Los Angeles: Cowman Publications, Inc. 1950), 94.

27. Mary O'Hara, quoted in Mrs. Chas. E. Cowman, *Consolation* (Los Angeles: Cowman Publications Inc. 1950), 192.

28. James Pryor, "A Letter To A Widow," 1868.

29. John Bunyan, *The Pilgrim's Progress* (New York, NY: The Heritage Press 1942), 49.

30. CS Lewis, "Myth Became Fact" *God in the Dock* (Grand Rapids, MI: Wm. B. Eerdmans Publishing 1972).

31. John Piper, *The Hidden Smile of God* (Wheaton, IL: Crossway 2001).

32. Dietrich Bonhoeffer, "Who Am I?"

33. Elizabeth Barrett Browning, "De Profundis," XXI.

34. Paul Tillich, *The Eternal Now*.

35. Quoted in Susan Duke, *Grieving Forward: Embracing Life Beyond Loss* (New York: Warner Faith 2006), 54.

36. Henri J. M. Nouwen, *Life of the Beloved* (New York: The Crossroad Publishing Company 2002).

37. Henry Van Dyke quoted in Mary Wilder Tileston, *Joy and Strength* (Minneapolis, MN: Worldwide Publications 1986), 189.

38. Jerry Sittser, *A Grace Disguised: How the Soul Grows Through Loss* (Grand Rapids, MI: Zondervan 1996), 56.

39. Frederick Buechner, *Listening to Your Life* (San Francisco, CA: Harper 1992), 287 quoted in Susan Duke, *Grieving Forward: Embracing Life Beyond Loss* (New York: Warner Faith 2006), 175.

40. Jerry Sittser, *A Grace Disguised: How the Soul Grows Through Loss* (Grand Rapids, MI: Zondervan 1996).

41. Ophelia G. Browning quoted in Mrs. Chas. E. Cowman, *Streams in the Desert* (Los Angeles, CA: The Oriental Missionary Society, 1946), 303.

42. Hugh Macmillan quoted in Ophelia G. Browning quoted in Mrs. Chas. E. Cowman, *Streams in the Desert* (Los Angeles, CA: The Oriental Missionary Society, 1946), 286.

43. J.R. Miller quoted in Al Bryant, *Climbing the Heights* (Grand Rapids, MI: Zondervan Publishing House 1956), 354.

44. Mrs. Chas. E. Cowman, *Consolation* (Los Angeles: Cowman Publications, Inc., 1950), 324.

45. Mrs. Chas. E. Cowman, *Streams in the Desert* (Los Angeles, CA: The Oriental Missionary Society, 1946), 352.

46. Martha Snell Nicholson, "The Thorn."

For information on how you can turn your writing into a book,
please contact Shawn Smucker at
shawnsmucker@yahoo.com